Individual Educational Programming for All Teachers of the Special Needs Learner

Individual Educational Programming for All Teachers of the Special Needs Learner

By

DONALD G. MYERS, Ed.D.

Associate Professor
Graduate Department of Special Education
Marywood College
Scranton, Pennsylvania

and

MICHAEL E. SINCO, Ed.D.

Director of Curriculum
Northeastern Intermediate Unit
Scranton, Pennsylvania

Lecturer, Marywood and Wilkes Colleges

CHARLES   C   THOMAS   •   PUBLISHER
Springfield · Illinois · U.S.A.

Published and Distributed Throughout the World by
CHARLES C THOMAS • PUBLISHER
Bannerstone House
301-327 East Lawrence Avenue, Springfield, Illinois, U.S.A.

© *1979, by* CHARLES C THOMAS • PUBLISHER
ISBN 0-398-03866-X
Library of Congress Catalog Card Number: 78-10908

Printed in the United States of America
V-R-1

Library of Congress Cataloging in Publication Data
Myers, Donald G
  Individual educational programming for all teachers of
the special needs learner.

  Includes index.
    1. Curriculum planning--United States. 2. Main-
streaming in education. 3. Language arts--United
States. 4. Arithmetic--Study and teaching--United
States. 5. Social sciences--Study and teaching--
United States. 6. Human ecology--Study and teaching--
United States. I. Sinco, Michael E., joint author.
II. Title.
LB1570.M93   375'.001'0973   78-10908
ISBN 0-398-03866-X

We wish to take this opportunity to express our deepest appreciation to our families for their encouragement and patient understanding while writing this book.

The Myerses: Elaine, Greg, Barry, Don, Beth, and Karen.

The Sincos: Ann, Michael, Stefan, Jennifer, and Jessica.

And, of course, our parents.

PREFACE

PUBLIC Law 94-142, enacted in 1977 as the Education for All Handicapped Children Act, scheduled for full implementation in fiscal year 1978, is blockbuster legislation. Schools in every part of the nation are destined to feel its impact. It opens the way for the schools in the United States to broaden their horizons, no longer focusing operations solely on "regular" students, but giving equal consideration to those with handicaps, including placing such youngsters in regular classrooms.

In an attempt to improve the training and performance of all teachers of handicapped and special needs students, we have developed an instructional program consisting of a series of skill areas and competencies to be developed by students through the teaching process. We have attempted to validate the curriculum's numerous instructional objectives and required competencies through imput from a cross section of teachers in the field and students directly involved in program participation.

The task of integrating the handicapped with the regular classroom system, referred to as "mainstreaming," has often been faced with the problem of mainstreaming curriculum consistency which must be transmitted between the special and regular educational programs. The achievement of mainstreaming is made possible with the use of our instructional approach.

Individual Educational Programming for Teachers of the Special Needs Learner was written with the hope of developing an educational communication system between regular and special teachers. We hope to take away the classification game used with children by building realistic, effective, life-oriented, individualized, instructional formats. Our intent is to put motivation back into the teaching-learning task by fashioning a curriculum that focuses on what students can do, rather than what they cannot do — an instructional approach open to innovation and individual talents of teachers; a program that documents learner progress, showing where the student was, where he is, and where he is going; and a classroom curriculum that contains information students desire and parents demand.

We hope this text will serve as a stimulus for teachers to think and develop their own instructional modifications in approach and objectives. We have not written this book as an end, but rather as a beginning.

Donald G. Myers
Michael E. Sinco

ACKNOWLEDGMENTS

WE wish to express our special appreciation to young Barry Myers for his graphic work that appears throughout the text. For a weightlifter he certainly has a nice touch.

D.G.M.
M.E.S.

CONTENTS

Individual Educational Programming for All Teachers of the Special Needs Learner

Chapter 1

INTRODUCTION

THE impressionable early school years constitute the base from which attitudes, habits, values, and later abstract, formal learnings grow. A comprehensive understanding of the needs of the young child should be reflected in the programs, methods, curricular materials, equipment, and organizational patterns forming the basis of each child's education.

Every child has an innate drive to understand the world in which he lives and to gain freedom and competence in it. Whatever the teacher can do to add to his understanding, his capacity for growth and pleasure, and his sense of freedom and dignity as an individual is of vital importance. Educators have come to realize that a person's needs, values, and feelings are important in the learning process; learning is highly personal.

The handicapped or special needs learner in the classroom is a great challenge to his teacher. Although he is more like other children than he is different, he is perhaps in need of more understanding than any other child. In our educational system he is no longer being neglected, but he continues to be misunderstood. Much time has been spent on trying to meet the mythical grade level or national norms in achievement. To the detriment of the special needs learner, conscientious teachers have devoted great amounts of time attempting to make something of the special needs learner that he is not capable of being. Today, when academic demands for achievement are being placed upon children to a degree never before thought possible, the special needs learner is in an even more vulnerable position.

The difficulties encountered by the special needs child begin early upon entry into school, in beginning reading, and even in the readiness program which precedes reading. Over the years

3

research studies have indicated that many slow learning children lack basic readiness skills which, it is often assumed, the average learning child brings with him when he enrolls in kindergarten or first grade. Since these skills are necessary for a major portion of the activities prescribed by the school, the child who has not developed them will find a large number of school tasks impossible. As the school year progresses, these special needs children fall each day further and further behind until they are no longer able to participate with the group in academic work.

It should be noted that the teacher spends a great deal of time with the special needs child. Much of this time could be more profitably spent by concentrating on pre-academic skills and a competency-based program of instruction, rather than the continued drilling on the academic activities, which are too difficult for the child to master. As a result of this misdirected instruction, the special needs learning child is frequently an unhappy person, facing defeat and failure. If he is not reached in the first year of school, his problem will increase in the second year, and his repeated failures become a vicious circle. The anticipation of failure is perhaps the most poignant aspect of underachievement. To expect failure is to almost assure oneself of constantly experiencing it in familial, academic, and social relationships.

The special needs learning child reveals to the teacher something of himself, his skills, his interests, his feelings, and his needs, not always in words, but through the language of behavior. The teacher must be constantly tuned to receive his signals and to respond to them in ways that will help him be his best self. Every child is different, and the teacher must recognize and accept these differences. The needs of each child should be considered unique; it is a challenge to the teacher to discover them and attempt to meet them in teaching.

The primary purpose of this book is to offer some basic suggestions and guides to the teacher, so that she may better prepare each child for a more rewarding academic life. The teacher should see that each child's abilities and skills are applied to meaningful activities and new learning experiences.

She must help the child develop his competencies as a student and as a valued person.

Successfully teaching the special needs learner requires the use of methods and techniques that stress ingenuity and creativity to stimulate the minds of youngsters who have not been previously awakened. The authors' plans are to suggest various competencies needed by all students and share some easily available or teacher-made activities. By this process we hope to provide constructive educational experiences for special needs learners in all classrooms.

Objectives

Chapter 2

THE OBJECTIVES

OVERVIEW: PUBLIC LAW 94-142

By any standards, Public Law 94-142, the Education for All Handicapped Children Act, is a law that promises an exciting new day for the 8 million handicapped children in this country and for educators concerned with their instruction. It opens the way for the nation's schools to broaden their horizons by giving equal consideration to those with handicaps or special needs. Placement of such children will be in regular classrooms to the fullest extent that doing so would be in their best interests.

Many of the advances called for in Public Law 94-142 have specific implications for the education of nonhandicapped students as well, two of which are especially noteworthy. The first, adopting a practice that enlightened educators have been advocating for many years, requires that children served by the Act be educated in accordance with individual plans tailored to their particular needs and capacities. The second calls for making what is now termed "preschool" education a standard part of the elementary level program, providing free public education to all handicapped children starting at age three.

Public Law 94-142 sets out to make certain that, without exception, every handicapped child in the United States (defined as "mentally retarded, hard of hearing, deaf, speech impaired, visually handicapped, seriously emotionally disturbed, orthopedically impaired, or other health impaired children, or youngsters with specific learning disabilities") receives "special education and related services." The major requirements of the Act are clearly worth noting and include the following:

A free public education will be made available to all handicapped children between the ages of three and eighteen by no later than September of 1978 and all those between three and twenty-one by September of 1980. Coverage of children in the three- to- five and eighteen- to- twenty-one ranges will not be required in states whose school attendance laws do not include those age brackets. Nevertheless, it is now national policy to begin the education of handicapped children by at least age three, and to encourage this practice Public Law 94-142 authorizes incentive grants of $300 over the regular allocation for each handicapped child between the ages of three and five who is afforded special education and related services.

For each handicapped child there will be an "individualized educational program." This will be a written statement jointly developed by a qualified school official, by the child's teacher, by the parents or guardian, and if possible, by the child himself. This written statement will include an analysis of the child's present achievement level, a listing of both short-range and annual goals, an identification of specific services that will be provided toward meeting those goals and an indication of the extent to which the child will be able to participate in regular school programs, a notation of when these services will be provided and how long they will last, and a schedule for checking on the progress being achieved under the plan and for making any revisions in it that seem to be called for.

Handicapped and nonhandicapped children will be educated together to the maximum extent appropriate, and the former will be placed in special classes or separate schools "only when the nature or severity of the handicap is such that education in regular classes," even if they are provided supplementary aids and services, "cannot be achieved satisfactorily."

Tests and other evaluation material used in placing handicapped children will be prepared and administered in such a way as not to be racially or culturally discriminatory, and they will be presented in the child's native tongue.

There will be an intensive and continuing effort to locate and identify youngsters who have handicaps, to evaluate their educational needs, and to determine whether those needs are being met.

In the overall effort to make sure education is available to all handicapped children, priority will be given first to those who are not receiving an education at all and second to those most severely handicapped within each disability who are receiving an inadequate education.

In school placement procedures and any decisions concerning a handicapped child's schooling, there will be prior consultation with the child's parents or guardian, and in general, no policies, programs, or procedures affecting the education of handicapped children covered by the law will be adopted without a public notice.

The rights and guarantees called for in the law will apply to handicapped children in private as well as public schools, and youngsters in private schools will be provided special education at no cost to their parents if the children were placed in these schools or referred to them by state or local education agency officials.

The states and localities will undertake comprehensive personnel development programs, including inservice training for regular as well as special education teachers and support personnel. Also, procedures will be launched for acquiring and disseminating information about promising educational practices and materials coming out of research and development efforts.

In implementing the law, special effort will be made to employ handicapped persons.

The principles set forth a few years ago in federal legislation that were aimed at the elimination of architectural barriers to the physically handicapped will be applied to school construction and modification, with authorized grants for these purposes.

The state education agency will have jurisdiction over all education programs for handicapped children offered within a given state, including those administered by a noneducation agency (a state hospital or the welfare department).

An advisory panel will be appointed by each governor to advise the state's education agency of unmet needs, comment publicly on such matters as proposed rules and regulations, and help the state develop and report relevant data. Membership on these panels will include handicapped individuals and parents or guardians of handicapped children.

Many of these policies have at one time or another been advocated by individual educators or by professional associations. Several have in fact been established within particular states, either by legislative action or as a consequence of court suits brought on behalf of handicapped children. In short, the concepts involved are not new. The difference is that through Public Law 94-142 they have become requirements, and accommodation to them is a condition of being eligible to receive support under the Act's funding provisions.

Action also might be taken by the parents of individual children, for Congress went to considerable pains to spell out various procedural safeguards. It is now required, for example, that parents or guardians have an opportunity to examine all relevant records bearing on the identification of children as being handicapped, on evaluating the nature and severity of their disability, and on the kind of educational setting in which they are placed. The latter issue is expected to be of particular concern to parents who feel their handicapped children have been unfairly denied access to regular classes. Schools are called upon to give written notice prior to changing a child's placement (and a written explanation if the school refuses a parent's request for such a change), and statements of this kind are to be in the parents' native tongue.

In the event of objections to a school's decision, there must be a process by which parents can register their complaints. That process must also include an opportunity for an impartial hearing which offers parents rights similar to those involved in a court case, such as the right to be advised by counsel (and by special education experts if they wish), to present evidence, to cross-examine witnesses, to compel the presence of any witnesses who do not appear voluntarily, to be provided a verbatim report of the proceedings, and to receive the decision and findings in written form.

Public Law 94-142 will most obviously affect the 10 to 12 percent of the school population who are handicapped, but its benefits will be felt by all other students as well and by all teachers and administrators. The fundamental promise of

Public Law 94-142 is that it will strengthen public education in general by strengthening what has been one of its weakest links. By opening classroom doors to all students, it will bring our schools far closer to the principles of democracy and justice on which the nation was founded.

CURRICULUM INTENT

The individual educational program curriculum for the special needs learner was prepared with certain goals in mind. First, and most important, is the goal of preparing each student for home life, community life, and work life. Second, this curriculum was designed to provide an individual plan of study for the learner. The third goal is to provide a comprehensive program that will meet the curriculum requirements leading to graduation.

The essence of the curriculum is practicality. In preparing the program, instructional objectives that facilitate effective integration into home, community, and work were given priority.

The Language Skills and Mathematics programs, after a developmental review, become essentially job-life oriented. The instructor who tries to use a theoretical or abstract approach in these areas will find teaching difficult, if not impossible. Therefore, practical needs are anticipated and used as motivation and material.

While the Language Skills program is a practical one and can easily be integrated with the other subjects, it must be recognized that all students may not achieve the reading facility hoped for. Therefore, it is most important that compensatory nonsymbolic techniques of instruction be utilized in the other subject areas. Field trips, films, filmstrips, picture books, recordings, and oral discussions should be as important as, or in many cases more important, than books. It is recommended that a filmstrip and cassette library corner be established for poor readers as a "free reading activity," in lieu of a library period.

The Human Ecology programs, which include health, safety,

and home economics, prepare the student for home life. Included in these programs are items that to some people are "common sense." Many of the child care, home, and personal emergency objectives fall into this category. It would be a mistake to assume that these "common sense" items need not be taught.

The Social Skills program was prepared not only with the aim of providing an understanding of the world and its communities, but also with the intent of preparing the student for a clearer understanding of his daily newspaper, the news on television, and the daily conversations of those with whom the learner comes in contact.

The Career and Vocational Skills program is of primary concern to the older, upper level student. It includes not only ways of getting and holding a job, but also related items such as using the money earned and surveying future educational possibilities.

The instructional objectives were designed to be as much help as possible to the instructor in preparing the teaching plans. To effectively use them, the instructor should first determine the number of sessions the objective will approximately require before it is achieved. The sections of the objective can then be broken down into class plans. Implied in each objective is the "given" providing the motivation and the "is able" providing the aim. Together they provide the evaluation which may be easily checked and recorded by the instructor. Also implied at the end of each objective is the phrase "to the satisfaction of the instructor." The objectives are not intended to be rigid and behavioral in content. A teacher or parent can easily comprehend a learner's program and observe progress simply by finding out whether the student meets the objectives.

It should be stressed that this curriculum is intended as a starting point. Objectives may eventually become more specific as instructors select materials and determine the varied needs of the learners. It should also be noted that a few of the objectives in a unit are very similar or even are repeated; this implies that the objectives are to be used in progression, from simple to more difficult. It is hoped that *given* the curriculum and the opportunity to select effective materials, the teacher *is able* to most effectively meet the needs of each individual student, thus preparing the learner for the fullest participation in his home, community, and life's work.

CURRICULUM IMPLEMENTATION

The following is an example of a special needs learner having difficulty in the mathematics area. The report includes the psychoeducational evaluation and the development of the Individual Educational Plan (IEP).

Case Study

Bobby, age nine years and four months, is presently repeating second grade. His teacher reports that he appears to be experiencing difficulty functioning independently in mathematics and reading.

In math Bobby's difficulty seems to be occurring in application and operations.

Bobby's teacher also reports that Bobby appears to be experiencing some difficulty interacting with his peers. His teacher feels that this situation may be due in part to his only limited success with group instruction, even with the basic skill group.

Psycho-Educational Evaluation

Stanford-Binet Intelligence Scale, Form L-M
   C.A.:   9-4
   M.A.:   7-0
Peabody Individual Achievement Test
   Mathematics   1.5
   Reading Recognition   1.4
   Reading Comprehension   below lowest level
   Spelling   1.5
Silvaroli Informal Reading Inventory
   Independent   — below lowest level
   Instructional   — readiness

Frustration — pre-primer
Detroit Test of Learning Aptitude
Auditory attention span for unrelated words — 4 yr.
Visual attention span for objects — 5 yr. 2 mo.
Auditory attention span for related syllables — 5 yr. 3 mo.
Visual attention span for letters — 6 yr. 6 mo.
Key Math Diagnostic Profile
Content — 1.4
Operations — 1.7
Application — 1.5

Following the psycho-educational evaluation a team conference was conducted. The team consisted of a psychologist, Bobby's classroom teacher, a learning disabilities consultant, the resource room teacher, a speech therapist, and a guidance

INFORMAL MATHEMATICS
SKILL ASSESSMENT

Name: **Bobby**   Date: **9-26-78**

(Count 20 blocks)

□ □ □ □ □ □ □ □ □ □ □ □ □ □ □ □ □ □ □ □

(Read numbers)

1   9   8   2   7   4   6   3   5

ADD (+)

```
                                              84
                                            2743
            5              23         254    614
   6        2      4       42    57   524     82
   1        1      7       37     7   173   6251
  ___      ___    ___     ___   ___   ___   ____
   7       (9)    (8)            (514)
```

SUBTRACT (−)

7	6	13	75	634	5203	500803
0	5	6	38	357	430	8017
⓪	④	⑬				

MULTUPLY (×)

4	18	612	742	628	614.3	7.382
2	4	5	8	207	2 7	3 .6

DIVIDE (÷)

4 ⟌8   7 ⟌49   3 ⟌694   4 ⟌9.302   31 ⟌8395   6.1 ⟌683   438 ⟌3852

ADD (+) REDUCE ALL FRACTIONS TO LOWEST TERMS.

	1/2		4 7/8	8 1/4
1/4	1/4	4 4/5	2 1/6	3 3/8
1/4	1/8	9 2/5	1 1/5	9 5/7

SUBTRACT (−)

5/8	4 3/4	5	8 2/5	18 1/4
2/8	2 3/4	1 4/7	5/8	13 2/3

MULTIPLY (×)

3/4 × 2/7 =   1/2 × 7 =   5/7 × 8/9 =   3 1/4 × 2/3 =   38 1/4
                                                                   12 1/2

Subtract	Divide	Average	Express in %	Write as a common fraction
8 xy	1/4 ÷ 2/3 =	38	2/3 =	
3 xy		82		6% =
	5/8 ÷ 3 1/2 =	67	.68 =	
		29		33 1/3% =
			13/100 =	

Write as a decimal fraction	Find	What % of 90 is 15?
5 1/2 =	120% of 40 =	Answer _____
		8 is 30% of what number?
4/7 =	3/4% of 500 =	Answer _____
7/100 =	5.8 % of 60 =	50 is what % of 600?
		Answer _____

counselor.

The team's report suggested that Bobby's educational program could be managed within the regular school setting without removing him from his present classroom. The team felt this could be accomplished by having Bobby take part in resource room instruction. Bobby would receive training in weak areas from the resource teacher and continue regular class instruction in his stronger areas.

In order to implement Bobby's plan a parent conference was conducted. The conference included Bobby's parents and the original members of the evaluation team. Bobby's parents agreed with the evaluation and the special needs placement. They also agreed to take part in the development of their son's individual educational plan.

Individual Educational Plan

What follows is an example of an Individual Educational Plan (IEP) developed for Bobby in mathematics, preceded by an Informal Mathematics Skill Assessment. Before Bobby's instructors could develop a plan for him in mathematics, it was necessary to determine his present level of educational performance. Formal psycho-educational evaluation is valuable, but it is recommended that the teacher develop and use an informal mathematics skill assessment to find Bobby's mathematics skill entry level. The teacher-made math assessment can assist the instructor in determining where Bobby should enter the curriculum.

SKILL PROFILE

Under Public Law 94-142, it may be expected that each special needs learner will have four or five regular education teachers, as well as at least one special educator. Federal law does not require that all the student's teachers develop the IEP. For this reason, some mechanism is necessary to insure

INDIVIDUAL EDUCATIONAL PLAN

NAME: Bobby DATE: 9-28-78

INSTRUCTIONAL AREA: Mathematics

ANNUAL GOAL: To improve Bobby's addition and subtraction skills.

CURRICULUM ENTRY: Math operations — demonstrate what happens when something is added or taken away from a group.

SHORT-TERM OBJECTIVE	EVALUATION PROCEDURES	CRITERIA OF SUCCESSFUL PERFORMANCE
1. Bobby will verbalize what happens when something is taken away from a group.	Given blocks, Bobby will place a prescribed number on a table and then add to and take away from a group.	95% accuracy
2. Bobby will solve addition problems to 6 using concrete objects.	Given addition problems to 6, Bobby will use an abacus to obtain the answers.	95% accuracy
3. Bobby will solve subtraction problems to 5 using concrete objects.	Given subtraction problems to 5, Bobby will use an abacus to obtain the answer.	95% accuracy
4. Bobby will supply the sums of the addition facts 1 through 5.	Given a worksheet of facts 1 through 5, Bobby will write the sums.	95% accuracy
5. Bobby will supply the sums of the addition facts 6 through 10.	Given a worksheet of facts 6 through 10, Bobby will write the sums.	95% accuracy
6. Bobby will solve addition problems using two digits with sums no more than 10.	Given a worksheet of addition problems with two digits, Bobby will write the sums.	95% accuracy

adequate and continued communication among all IEP implementers and the exchange of important information.

The Skill Profile was designed to assist teachers who frequently need more than the standardized psycho-educational testing, which seldom provides information that can be used in developing programming strategies.

The profile is composed of five major skill areas: language, mathematics, human ecology, social, and career — vocational. Contained within each skill area is a varying number of subscales with instructional objectives which make up the curriculum content.

We believe one of the best ways to determine a student's skills is to compare his or her present abilities against comprehensive sequences of skills. All skill sequences are presented in the curriculum as instructional objectives. The objectives begin at the most basic level and progress to competent functioning in major academic and living skill areas.

The Skill Profile is not a standardized or validated instrument. It is intended as an informal device to assist the instructional process — to supplement, not replace, formalized evaluations.

The profile may be used at any time to determine present skill levels, assess specific strengths or limitations, and project skills to work on. It will frequently be used to follow standard school grading periods or in response to parent requests. The information may be used by all instructional personnel to maintain consistency in programming. Placing each learner within a sequence of skills permits the formulation of a basic measurement of where the student is and what skills might be suitable for instruction.

The Skill Profile attempts to assess the learner's present range of skills. The graph consists of all the skill areas with the number on the graph corresponding to the number in the curriculum instructional objectives. Subscale skill areas vary in the number of items to be achieved. For example, there are 435 reading objectives and only 10 objectives in the telephone skill sequence. When an item is presented during instruction and the learner demonstrates competency, to the satisfaction of the teacher, it can then be noted on the profile graph. In this manner the instructional items are used in evaluation and instruction simultaneously. The graph provides a visual review of the learner's current skill levels. It also allows easy review of the learner's general developmental patterns.

SKILL PROFILE

Academic - - Living Skills

SKILL LEVEL	Language Skills		Mathematics Skills			Human Ecology						Social Skills				Career and Vocational Skills								
	Language	Reading	Numeration	Operations	Measurement	Health	Safety	Food	Clothing	Child Care	Home Emergencies	Social Beginnings	Local-State Community	National Community	World Community	World of Work	Telephone Skills	Money-Tax-Bank-Insurance	Locating a Job	Employment	Home Management	Leisure-Recreation	Greenhouse	Landscaping
100%	115	435	117	140	170	54	29	48	36	22	14	16	30	34	26	30	10	48	25	22	20	12	78	58
75%	86	326	88	105	128	40	22	36	27	16	10	12	22	26	20	22	8	36	19	16	15	9	58	44
50%	58	218	58	70	85	27	14	24	18	11	7	8	15	17	13	15	5	24	12	11	10	6	39	29
25%	29	109	29	35	42	14	7	12	9	6	4	4	8	8	6	8	3	12	6	6	5	3	20	14

Mark the number of each item completed correctly. Work up from starting item no. 1 to final item number. Each evaluation can be distinguished by using different colors to illustrate learner progress.

Chapter 3

THE CURRICULUM
Unit I

LANGUAGE
SKILLS

THE language skills program was designed to provide the student with a program of developmental reading as well as an understanding of the basic skills in oral and written expression. It is expected that the student will acquire a familiarity with the basic spelling word lists. At this point, spelling words can be selected from the student's classroom activities. For the student who has limited reading ability, the teacher will, of necessity, spend considerable time on the sequential behavioral objectives in reading itemized in the curriculum.

In the upper level, the program becomes essentially practical and job-life oriented. During this period of time, the student, preparing for an occupation and possibly participation in a work-study program, should feel a need to read, write, and build vocabulary in areas of his practical experiences.

It must be kept in mind that the instructional objectives listed do not comprise an all-inclusive list. Since many are based on the real life activities of the student at home, in the school, or on the job, many others will suggest themselves. The broader the base of students life-oriented learning experiences, the more extensive will be opportunities for learning in the language skills.

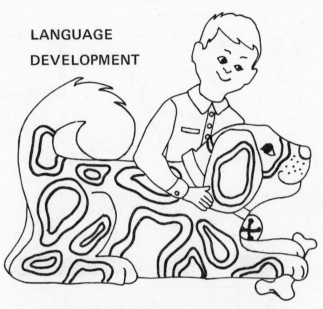

LANGUAGE
DEVELOPMENT

ITEM   INSTRUCTIONAL OBJECTIVE

Pre-Language Skills
The student is able to . . .
1. Sit at least thirty seconds.
2. Tract objects visually.
3. Look at objects upon command.
4. Locate sounds.
5. Perform gross motor tasks on command (stand-up, sit-down, roll-ball, kick-ball, and other single-action tasks).
6. Point to body parts (eyes, mouth, nose, ear, etc.).
7. Perform gestures of communication (bye-bye, peek-a-boo, pat-a-cake, etc.).
8. Respond to name.
9. Respond to "no."
10. Follow simple one-stage commands (come, go).
11. Identify objects by pointing.

Figure 1. Communication Board No. 1 provides illustrations of specific needs (drink, elimination, entertainment) which the student can identify by pointing.

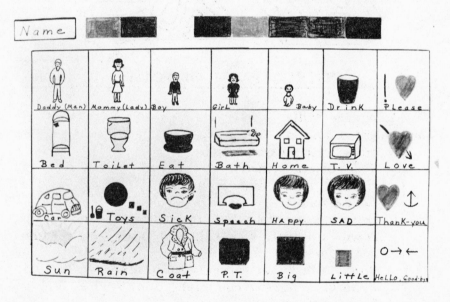

Figure 2. Communication Board No. 2 demonstrates the ability of a student to identify higher level needs by matching pictures or abstract symbols with single words or phrases.

ITEM   INSTRUCTIONAL OBJECTIVE

The student is able to . . .

12. Discriminate between objects by pointing.
13. Recognize at least one simple contrast-pair by pointing (big — little).
14. Recognize primary colors (red, blue, yellow, etc.)

(For students developing language skills the use of communication boards may be of assistance. Examples are provided, but teachers should be encouraged to develop their own to meet the special needs of the students.)

15. Communicate needs by pointing to the specific illustration (to drink, to eliminate, to be entertained; *see* Fig. 1).
16. Communicate higher level needs by pointing to the specific pictures (*see* Fig. 2).

LANGUAGE SKILLS

17. Respond to familiar environmental sounds.
18. Listen attentively to a short story.
19. Use a declarative sentence. (This is a cup. The cup is blue.)
20. Say a sentence using the correct verb form.
21. Use the correct form of a noun, singular or plural, when saying a sentence.
22. Produce the long vowel sounds and less difficult consonants in imitation.
23. Verbalize common nouns and action verbs.
24. Verbalize his personal needs.
25. Begin to use suitable, courteous expressions (thank you, please).
26. Given a two-step command, carry out the actions correctly. (Close the door. Return to your seat.)
27. Listen to a short story and answer *yes* and *no* questions related to the story.
28. Complete simple oral analogies. (Sock is to foot as

ITEM	INSTRUCTIONAL OBJECTIVE

The student is able to . . .

glove is to _____ .)

29. Demonstrate that he understands the positive form of adjectives of size by following oral directions containing adjectives. (Pick up the big block.)

30. Demonstrate that he understands the directional prepositions by following oral instructions containing prepositions.

31. Demonstrate an understanding of quantitative adjectives by following oral instructions containing adjectives.

32. Demonstrate an understanding of basic adverbs by following directions containing adverbs.

33. Given pictures representing concrete nouns, sort the pictures into categories.

34. Use the words *is* and *are* with the correct forms of nouns in sentences.

35. Begin to use the past tense of verbs in sentences.

36. Participate in simple conversation.

37. Use courteous expressions.

38. Enunciate the vowels and the easier consonants.

39. Cultivate an oral vocabulary containing simple descriptive and quantitative adjectives.

40. Practice good listening manners.

41. Listen to a short story and remember one event.

42. Demonstrate an understanding of opposites. Given a word, the student is able to name a word with the opposite meaning (stop — go).

43. Demonstrate an understanding of comparative and superlative adjectives of size by following oral directions containing adjectives.

44. Demonstrate an understanding of more abstract nouns, such as happiness, by correctly identifying pictures.

45. Demonstrate an understanding of the meanings of less concrete action verbs, such as carry, by following oral

ITEM INSTRUCTIONAL OBJECTIVE

The student is able to . . .

directions.

46. Demonstrate an understanding of the meanings of possessive pronouns by identifying objects that are his, hers, its, and theirs.

47. Given pictures of objects, categorize the objects as to function.

48. Ask a question using correct sentence structure.

49. Use expanded declarative sentences incorporating prepositional phrases.

50. Begin to use the future tense of verbs in sentences.

51. Participate in making daily plans.

52. Orally extend an invitation.

53. Enunciate consonants correctly.

54. Use abstract nouns and less common action verbs in sentences.

55. Use possessive pronouns and simple prepositions in sentences.

56. Given a three-step command, carry out the actions correctly. (Put the pencil on the desk, close the door, and bring me your book.)

57. Demonstrate an understanding of simple similarities and differences by telling ways objects are similar and different in color, size, and shape.

58. Demonstrate an understanding of the meaning of personal pronouns by completing sentences orally that use personal pronouns. (Who has the blue coat? *She* has the blue coat.)

59. Given a category, name concrete nouns that belong in the category.

60. Tell if a statement about an object is true or false. (The ball is square.)

61. Use expanded declarative sentences with a compound subject and/or object.

62. Begin to use correctly the past tense of irregular verbs.

63. Participate in a small group discussion.

ITEM	INSTRUCTIONAL OBJECTIVE

The student is able to . . .

64. Make a courteous introduction. (Mrs. Jones, this is my mother.)
65. Use courteous telephone manners.
66. Use conjunctions appropriately in sentences.
67. Use comparative and superlative adjectives in sentences.
68. Cultivate an oral vocabulary containing descriptive, quantitative, comparative, and superlative adjectives.
69. Listen to a short story and remember the events that happened in the story.
70. Demonstrate an understanding of abstract similarities and differences by stating ways objects are similar in function and composition.
71. Demonstrate an understanding of abstract verbs by following oral directions containing abstract verbs. (Point to the picture that shows a child who is thinking.)
72. Demonstrate an understanding of abstract adjectives and adverbs by following oral directions containing abstract adjectives and adverbs. (Point to the small girl who is playing happily.)
73. Given a group of pictures of objects, categorize the pictures according to source.
74. Listen to a statement and tell if it is true or false.
75. Use sentence structure that incorporates adjectives and personal pronouns.
76. Use the passive mood of verbs correctly.
77. Make a short speech before a group about a personal experience.
78. Correctly enunciate consonants, consonant blends, and consonant digraphs.
79. Combine consonants and vowels to make familiar words.
80. Given a four-step command, carry out the actions correctly.

ITEM	INSTRUCTIONAL OBJECTIVE

The student is able to . . .

81. Listen to a story and summarize the events in correct sequence.
82. Demonstrate an understanding of abstract relationships by correctly matching pictures of objects (road — car, sidewalk — person).
83. Given a word, name homonyms of that word.
84. Categorize abstract words.
85. Tell why an abstract statement is true or false.
86. Use sentence structure that incorporates adverbs.
87. Use sentence structure that incorporates the past participle of a verb with an auxiliary verb.
88. Make an oral presentation to a group using a logical sequence.
89. Summarize an experience accurately.
90. Give a simple definition of a word.
91. Listen to a story and relate detailed information about the story.
92. Demonstrate the ability to make abstract analogies by correctly completing oral sentences. (Hand is to clap as voice is to _____ .)
93. Name synonyms of common words.
94. Categorize items according to two criteria.
95. Supply a logical ending to an unfinished story.
96. Use compound sentence structure that incorporates coordinating conjunctions.
97. Use all tenses of common verbs correctly.
98. Given two sentences orally, select the one that is grammatically preferable.
99. Talk before a group.
100. Give detailed information and directions correctly.
101. Use synonyms when defining words.
102. Follow complex directions correctly.
103. Remember and relate preceding events in a continuous story.
104. Complete difficult analogies by correctly completing

ITEM	INSTRUCTIONAL OBJECTIVE

The student is able to . . .

oral sentences. (Paper clip is to paper as pin is to
_____ .)

105. Name antonyms of common words.

106. Explain the relationship between items in a series and complete the series.

107. Use complex sentence structure.

108. Use the subjunctive mood of verbs correctly.

109. Write a short business letter.

110. Fill out job applications.

111. Fill out an application for a driver's license.

112. Write a letter applying for a job.

113. Write a letter requesting information.

114. Write an original short story.

115. Write an original rhyme or short poem.

READING

INSTRUCTIONAL UNIT

ITEM	INSTRUCTIONAL OBJECTIVE

PRE-READING SKILLS

The student is able to . . .

1. Sit and attend for seven minutes.
2. Recognize and respond to his own name.
3. Listen to a simple story.
4. Recognize visual likenesses and match identical objects.
5. Identify like objects from a group.
6. Recognize differences; from a group, the student is able to select one object that is different.

ITEM   INSTRUCTIONAL OBJECTIVE

The student is able to . . .

7. Name familiar objects in the classroom.
8. Discriminate primary colors and match objects.
9. Discriminate sizes by matching large and small circles or squares.
10. Verbalize a simple answer to a question.
11. Understand and respond to action words (run, sit, hop).
12. Answer questions emphasizing verbs. (Is the dog running?)
13. Answer questions emphasizing subjects and verbs. (Who is running?)
14. Ask basic questions.
15. Discriminate between loud and soft sounds.
16. Repeat series of three words.
17. Relate an experience to the class using complete sentences.
18. Repeat series of three words in order.
19. Repeat series of three sounds.
20. Reproduce a basic drawing.
21. Reproduce a drawing after it is removed from view.
22. Draw a line from left to right.
23. Color, demonstrating left to right progression.
24. Proceed from top to bottom when coloring a column of objects.
25. Supply the missing object to a drawing.
26. Recognize the main idea in a picture story.
27. Recognize first, last, and middle places in a series of objects.
28. Select objects from a drawing that can be classified together.
29. Tell the story content of a picture.
30. Tell the sequence of events in correct order.
31. Arrange four pictures in a story sequence.
32. Locate a given word on a chart.
33. From a series of pictures, predict the outcome of story.

ITEM   INSTRUCTIONAL OBJECTIVE

READING SKILLS
The student is able to . . .

34-45. Discriminate auditorily the initial phonemes b, d, f, g, h, k, l, m, r, s, t, and w.

46-53. Select drawings of objects beginning with c, d, f, k, m, r, t, and w.

54, 56, 58, 60, 62, 64, 66. Produces the sounds of letters c, d, f, k, m, r, and t, when shown graphic forms of letters.

55, 57, 59, 61, 63, 65, 67. Identify words in his sight vocabulary that begin with c, d, f, k, m, r, and t, when given pictures of objects beginning with those letters.

68.   Using a basic sight word list (dolch), classify words beginning with c, d, f, k, m, r, and t.

69.   Match four words with their configuration.

70.   Read a sentence with one unknown word whose meaning is determined from context.

71.   Recognize known words to which "s" has been added.

72.   Make auditory distinction between singular and plural nouns and select the matching printed word.

73.   Adds "s" to known nouns to form plurals.

74.   Understand the meaning of next, beginning, and end in a series of objects.

75.   Repeat a sequence of five words.

76.   Compose basic reading materials through chalkboard and experience charts.

77.   Classify nine objects into three groups according to function.

78.   Locate beginning and ending of a sentence in a chart story.

79.   Given four words, select one *not* related (dog, cat, *house,* bird).

80.   Answer five questions composed of sight words, by indicating *yes* or *no.*

81.   Given four word cards, assemble a sentence.

82.   Construct a sentence with word cards to match a sentence on the board.

ITEM	INSTRUCTIONAL OBJECTIVE

The student is able to . . .

83. Read two pages from a reading book and answer two questions correctly.

84. Read a story in a reading book.

85. Read an unfamiliar story composed of basic sight words.

86. From five sentences relating to a story in a reader, indicate if a statement is correct by marking *yes* or *no*.

87. Organize ideas into language units by telling a story using a sequence of pictures.

88. Relate a story to his own experiences by telling a related personal incident.

89. Using the same story, tell how he would be if he were the character in the story.

90. Locate the title of a book.

91. Locate the title of a story.

92. Locate the table of contents in a book.

93. Discriminate rhyming words (ring, sing).

94. Recognize likenesses and differences in initial sounds.

95. Given a printed word, identify the same word in a line of similar words.

96. Given a drawing of an object that begins with "b," select other drawings of objects beginning with the same sound.

97. Given a drawing of an object that begins with "g" (guh), select other drawings of objects beginning with the same sounds.

98. Given a drawing of an object that begins with "h," select other drawings of objects beginning with the same sound.

99. Given a drawing of an object that begins with "j," select other drawings of objects beginning with the same sound.

100. Given a drawing of an object that begins with "l," select other drawings of objects beginning with the same sound.

ITEM   INSTRUCTIONAL OBJECTIVE

The student is able to . . .

101. Given a drawing of an object that begins with "n," select other drawings of objects beginning with the same sound.
102. Given a drawing of an object that begins with "p," select other drawings of objects beginning with the same sound.
103. Given a drawing of an object that begins with "s," select other drawings of objects beginning with the same sound.
104. Given a drawing of an object that begins with "v," select other drawings of objects beginning with the same sound.
105. Given a drawing of an object that begins with "w," select other drawings of objects beginning with the same sound.
106. Given a drawing of an object that begins with "y," select other drawings of objects beginning with the same sound.
107. Given a drawing of an object that begins with "z," select other drawings of objects beginning with the same sound.
108. From four words presented orally, select the one word that does not begin with the same sound.
109. Identify the sound of the letter "b."
110. Given a picture of an object that begins with "b" and the letter "b," identify words in sight vocabulary that begin with "b."
111. Identify the sound of the letter "g" (guh).
112. Given a picture of an object that begins with "g" (guh) and the letter "g," identify words in sight vocabulary that begin with "g."
113. Identify the sound of the letter "h."
114. Given a picture of an object that begins with "h" and the letter "h," identify words in sight vocabulary that begin with "h."

ITEM	INSTRUCTIONAL OBJECTIVE

The student is able to . . .

115. Identify the sound of the letter "j."
116. Given a picture of an object that begins with "j" and the letter "j," identify words in sight vocabulary that begin with "j."
117. Identify the sound of the letter "l."
118. Given a picture of an object that begins with "l" and the letter "l," identify words in sight vocabulary that begin with "l."
119. Identify the sound of the letter "n."
120. Given a picture of an object that begins with "n" and the letter "n," identify words in sight vocabulary that begin with "n."
121. Identify the sound of the letter "p."
122. Given a picture of an object that begins with "p" and the letter "p," identify words in sight vocabulary that begin with "p."
123. Identify the sound of the letter "s."
124. Given a picture of an object that begins with "s" and the letter "s," identify words in sight vocabulary that begin with "s."
125. Identify the sound of the letter "v."
126. Given a picture of an object that begins with "v" and the letter "v," identify words in sight vocabulary that begin with "v."
127. Identify the sound of the letter "w."
128. Given a picture of an object that begins with "w" and the letter "w," identify words in sight vocabulary that begin with "w."
129. Identify the sound of the letter "y."
130. Given a picture of an object that begins with "y" and the letter "y," identify words in sight vocabulary that begin with "y."
131. Identify the sound of the letter "z."
132. Given a picture of an object that begins with "z" and the letter "z," identify words in sight vocabulary that

ITEM	INSTRUCTIONAL OBJECTIVE

The student is able to . . .

begin with "z."

133. Given six cards containing the printed letters "b," "g," "h," "j," "l," and "n," indicate the beginning sounds of words pronounced by holding up the correct letter.

134. Given six cards containing the printed letters "p," "s," "v," "w," "y," and "z," indicate the beginning sounds of words pronounced by holding up the correct letter.

135. Given the letters "b," "g," "h," "l," "j," "m," and pictures of objects, correctly match the object and the beginning sound.

136. Given the letters "p," "s," "v," "w," "y," "z," and pictures of objects, correctly match the object and the beginning sound.

137. Given a page containing pairs of words that rhyme, match the words that rhyme.

138. Select the singular or plural correct form to be inserted in a sentence composed of basic sight words.

139. Select the correct form of a verb (run, runs) to be inserted in sentences composed of basic sight words.

140. Add "s" to a known word (noun or verb) and state an oral sentence correctly using the newly formed word.

141. Given four letters, both capital and lower case, select the letter sound pronounced.

142. Name an object in a picture and state a complete sentence using the object word.

143. Given a drawing of nine objects, make three groups of similar objects.

144. Given a list of seven nouns and seven short descriptions, match each noun with the correct descriptive phrase.

145. Given three phrase strips, arrange the phrases to make a sentence.

146. Given four sets of phrases, match the beginning

ITEM	INSTRUCTIONAL OBJECTIVE

The student is able to . . .

phrases with the correct ending phrases to form four sentences.

147. Read and answer six questions composed of sight words by writing *yes* or *no*.

148. Recognize a period and demonstrate its use in a sentence.

149. Recognize a question mark and demonstrate its use in a sentence.

150. Compose a complete sentence for a picture.

151. Given six simple sentences related to a story in a reading book, designate if the statement is correct by marking *yes* or *no*.

152. Demonstrate the ability to recall details in a story read by correctly answering questions.

153. Accurately relate a story.

154. Given three sentences, select the one that tells the main idea of a story.

155. Given a question, locate a sentence in a story that states the answer.

156. Given a sentence telling the first event in a story, identify additional sequential events.

157. Demonstrate the ability to anticipate outcomes in a reading by suggesting events that could happen next.

158. Correctly respond to a series of oral directions.

159. Carry out an oral message.

160. Read the words spoken by a character in a story.

161. Use the table of contents to read titles of stories and to locate stories in the book using the page numbers.

162. Given a word orally that ends with "d," "k," "l," or "m," identify the final consonant.

163. Given a word orally that ends with "n," "p," "r," or "t," identify the final consonant.

164. Identify the sound of the consonant digraph "ch." Given a picture of an object that begins with "ch" and the letters "ch," identify words in sight vocabulary

ITEM   INSTRUCTIONAL OBJECTIVE

The student is able to . . .

that begin with "ch."

165. Identify the sound of the consonant digraph "sh." Given a picture of an object that begins with "sh" and the letters "sh," identify words in sight vocabulary that begin with "sh."

166. Identify the sound of the consonant digraph "th" (voiced). Given a picture of an object that begins with "th" (voiced) and the letters "th," identify words in sight vocabulary that begin with "th."

167. Identify the sound of the consonant digraph "th" (unvoiced). Given a picture of an object that begins with "th" (unvoiced) and the letters "th," identify words in sight vocabulary that begin with "th."

168. Identify the sound of the consonant digraph "wh." Given a picture of an object that begins with "wh" and the letters "wh," identify words in sight vocabulary that begin with "wh."

169. Identify the sound of consonant digraphs in which one letter is silent (ck, gn, kn, wr). Given a picture of an object that ends with "ck," identify words in sight vocabulary that end with "ck."

170. Given a picture of an object that ends with "ch" and the letters "ch," identify words in sight vocabulary that end with "ch."

171. Given a picture of an object that ends with "sh" and the letters "sh," identify words in sight vocabulary that end with "sh."

172. Given a picture of an object that ends with "th" and the letters "th," identify words in sight vocabulary that end with "th."

173. Blend together the sounds of two or more consonants so that the sound of neither is lost.

174. Identify the sound of the consonant blends "bl" and "br." Given a picture of objects that begin with "bl" and "br," identify words in sight vocabulary that

ITEM	INSTRUCTIONAL OBJECTIVE

The student is able to . . .

begin with "bl" and "br."

175. Identify the sound of the consonant blends "cl" and "cr." Given a picture of objects that begin with "cl" and "cr," identify words in sight vocabulary that begin with "cl" and "cr."

176. Identify the sound of the consonant blend "dr." Given a picture of an object that begins with "dr," identify words in sight vocabulary that begin with "dr."

177. Identify the sound of the consonant blends "fl" and "fr." Given a picture of objects that begin with "fl" and "fr," identify words in sight vocabulary that begin with "fl" and "fr."

178. Identify the sound of the consonant blends "gl" and "gr." Given a picture of objects that begin with "gl" and "gr," identify words in sight vocabulary that begin with "gl" and "gr."

179. Identify the sound of the consonant blends "pl" and "pr." Given a picture of objects that begin with "pl" and "pr," identify words in sight vocabulary that begin with "pl" and "pr."

180. Identify the sound of the consonant blends "sc," "sk," "sl," and "sm." Given a picture of objects that begin with "sc," "sk," "sl," and "sm," identify words in sight vocabulary that begin with each blend.

181. Identify the sound of the consonant blends "sn," "sp," "st," and "sw." Given a picture of objects that begin "sn," "sp," "st," and "sw," identify words in sight vocabulary that begin with each blend.

182. Identify the sound of the consonant blend "tr." Given a picture of an object that begins with "tr," identify words in sight vocabulary that begin with "tr."

183. Identify the sound of the consonant blend "st" when it comes at the end of a word. Given a picture of an object that ends with "st," identify words in sight vocabulary that end with "st."

ITEM	INSTRUCTIONAL OBJECTIVE

The student is able to . . .

184. Given a list of words having the same common phonogram (at, in, ot, an, en, ay, et), select the word pronounced (cat, mat, rat, fat, bat, etc.).

185. Given a list of words containing the phonograms "at," "in," "ot," "an," "en," "ay," and "et," list the words under these elements and pronounce each word.

186. Given a list of words having the same common phonogram (ill, all, un), select the word pronounced.

187. Given a list of words containing the phonograms "ill," "all," and "un," list the words under these elements and pronounce each word.

188. Given a list of words having the same common phonogram (old, ing, ell, ow, ake), select the word pronounced.

189. Given a list of words containing the phonograms "old," "ing," "ell," "ow," and "ake," list the words under these elements and pronounce each word.

190. Given words containing the phonograms "at," "in," "ot," "an," "en," "ay," and "et," use initial consonant substitution to form new words.

191. Given words containing the phonograms "ill," "all," and "un," use initial consonant substitution to form new words.

192. Given words containing the phonograms "old," "ing," "ell," "ow," and "ake," use initial consonant substitution to form new words.

193. Change the initial consonant in a word to form a new word.

194. Change the final consonant in a word to form a new word.

195. Add "ed" to a known word and correctly make an oral sentence using the new word correctly.

196. Add "es" to a word to form the plural.

197. Add "ing" to a known verb and state an oral sentence correctly using the newly formed word.

ITEM	INSTRUCTIONAL OBJECTIVE

The student is able to . . .

198. Given a written sentence composed of known words and a blank, fill in the blank with the correct form of the word, the root word, or the root word with "ing" added.

199. Understand the possessive form of known words. Given a sentence containing a possessive form of a known noun, read the sentence and interpret its meaning.

200. Add "s" to a known word to form the possessive.

201. Given written sentences composed of known words and blanks, fill in the blanks with correct possessives.

202. Identify a compound word (something, sunshine, sometime, everything, airplane) and tell the words from which it was formed.

203. Given a list of eight words (some, air, grand, sun, thing, plane, father, shine), form four compound words.

204. Read simple contractions (don't, I'll, let's) and tell the words from which the contractions were formed.

205. Given three sets of two words (do not, I will, let us), form and write three contractions.

206. Given a list of eight nouns and eight short descriptions, match each noun with the correct descriptive phrase.

207. Given six words and six sentences composed of known words and blanks, write in the correct word for each sentence.

208. Read statements with the correct inflection.

209. Read an interrogative sentence using the correct inflection.

210. Compose and state an interrogative sentence.

211. Recognize a comma and demonstrate its use in a sentence.

212. Read a sentence containing a comma using the correct inflection.

ITEM	INSTRUCTIONAL OBJECTIVE

The student is able to . . .

213. Recognize quotation marks and demonstrate their use in a sentence.

214. Read a sentence that contains quotation marks using the correct inflection.

215. Identify the speakers in a story.

216. Recognize an exclamation mark and demonstrate its use in a sentence.

217. Read sentences using proper inflection to indicate excitement and happiness.

218. Read and answer eight questions composed of sight words by writing *yes* or *no.*

219. Given four sentences related to a story in a reading book, designate if the statement is correct by marking *yes* or *no.*

220. Demonstrate the ability to recall details in a story read by correctly answering three out of four questions asked.

221. Given three sentences, select the one that tells the main idea of a story that was read.

222. When asked a question, locate and read a sentence from a story that states the answer.

223. Given three sentences that tell events in a story, number the sentences in sequential order.

224. Demonstrate that he recognizes the feelings of story characters by telling how he thinks the characters feel.

225. Use the table of contents to locate a specific story.

226. Demonstrate the ability to anticipate outcomes from a reading by indicating events that could happen next.

227. Distinguish fact from fiction. Given ten sentences, mark the facts *yes* and the fictitious statements *no.*

228. Compare and contrast two characters in a story.

229. Given a list of sight vocabulary words, group the words as living and nonliving things.

230. Given a list of sight vocabulary words, group the words as things to touch and things to do.

ITEM	INSTRUCTIONAL OBJECTIVE

The student is able to . . .

231. Classify words as those that name things and as words that describe.

232. Read a series of events and conclude the story in his own words.

233. Identify the two sounds of the letter "f" when it comes at the end of a word (of, off).

234. Given a word orally that ends with "f," identify the final consonant.

235. Identify the sound of the consonant blend "chr."

236. Given a picture of an object that begins with "chr," identify words that begin with "chr."

237. Identify the sound of the consonant blend "scr."

238. Given a picture of an object that begins with "scr," identify words that begin with "scr."

239. Identify the sound of the consonant blend "shr."

240. Given a picture of an object that begins with "shr," identify words that begin with "shr."

241. Identify the sound of the consonant blend "str."

242. Given a picture of an object that begins with "str," identify words that begin with "str."

243. Identify the sound of the consonant blend "thr."

244. Given a picture of an object that begins with "thr," identify words that begin with "thr."

245. Identify the sound of the consonant blend "qu," and correctly pronounce words that begin with "qu."

246. Identify the sound of the consonant blend "tw."

247. Given a picture of an object that begins with "tw," identify words that begin with "tw."

248. Name the vowels (a, e, i, o, u).

249. Demonstrate an awareness that "y" may be used as a vowel. Identify "y" as the vowel in words where "y" has the "i" or "e" sound.

250. Reproduce the long sound of the vowels.

251. Name a key word for each vowel that has the long sound (cake, boat, etc.).

ITEM	INSTRUCTIONAL OBJECTIVE

The student is able to . . .

252. Given a list of one syllable words, circle the words having the long sound of "a."

253. Given a list of one syllable words, circle the words having the long sound of "e."

254. Given a list of one syllable words, circle the words having the long sound of "o."

255. Given a list of one syllable words, circle the words having the long sound of "u."

256. Given a list of one syllable words, circle the words having the long sound of "i."

257. Reproduce the short sound of the vowels.

258. Name a key word for each vowel that has the short sound (cat, bed, pig, pot, cup).

259. Given a list of one syllable words, circle the words having the short sound of "a."

260. Given a list of one syllable words, circle the words having the short sound of "e."

261. Given a list of one syllable words, circle the words having the short sound of "i."

262. Given a list of one syllable words, circle the words having the short sound of "o."

263. Given a list of one syllable words, circle the words having the short sound of "u."

264. Write one column of words containing the long sound of the vowel "a" and another column containing the short sound of the vowel "a."

265. Write one column of words containing the long sound of the vowel "e" and another column containing the short sound of the vowel "e."

266. Write one column of words containing the long sound of the vowel "i" and another column containing the short sound of the vowel "i."

267. Write one column of words containing the long sound of the vowel "o" and another column containing the short sound of the vowel "o."

ITEM	INSTRUCTIONAL OBJECTIVE

The student is able to . . .

268. Write one column of words containing the long sound of the vowel "u" and another column containing the short sound of the vowel "u."

269. Given a list of words containing the diphthong "oi," identify the letters representing the sound of "oi" in the word "coin."

270. Given a list of words containing the diphthong "ou," identify the letters representing the sound of "ou" in the word "loud."

271. Reproduce the sounds of the diphthongs "oi" and "ou" and pronounce nonsense syllables containing the diphthongs.

272. Given a list of words having the same common phonogram "ook," select the word pronounced.

273. Given a list of words having the same common phonogram "ight," select the word pronounced.

274. Given a list of words containing the phonograms "ook," "ight," and "ould," pronounce each word.

275. Substitute initial consonant digraphs (wh, sh, th, ch) for the initial consonants in known words to form new words.

276. Substitute final consonant digraphs (ch, ck, sh, th, ng) for the final consonants in known words to form new words.

277. Substitute initial consonant blends for the initial consonants in known words to form new words.

278. Pronounce short words ending in "e" preceded by a consonant where the "e" is usually silent and the preceding vowel sound is long (home, game).

279. Pronounce words where two vowels come together and usually the first is long and the second is silent.

280. Sound single vowel words ending in a consonant where the vowel sound is short.

281. Pronounce single vowel letter words followed by the letter "r," when controlling the vowel sound.

ITEM	INSTRUCTIONAL OBJECTIVE

The student is able to . . .

282. Add "y" to a known word.

283. Locate and differentiate between plurals and possessives.

284. Add "ly" to a known word and use the inflectional form correctly in a sentence.

285. Add "er" and "est" to a known word (cold, colder, coldest) and use all — root, comparative, and superlative — forms correctly in sentences.

286. Add the suffix "er" to a known word, tell the meaning of the word, and use the word correctly in a sentence.

287. Add the suffix "ness" to a known word, tell the meaning of the word, and use the word correctly in a sentence.

288. Double the final consonant in a word before adding a suffix.

289. Drop the final "e" from a word before adding a suffix.

290. Add the prefix "un" to a known word, tell the meaning of the new word, and use the word correctly in a sentence.

291. Add the prefix "dis" to a known word, tell the meaning of the new word, and use the word correctly in a sentence.

292. Add the prefix "re" to a known word, tell the meaning of the new word, and use the word correctly in a sentence.

293. Alphabetize words by using the initial letters.

294. Given two words from a word list and ten sentences with blanks, write in the correct word for each sentence.

295. Given a list of ten words from a word list and ten brief definitions, match each word with the correct definition.

296. Given six sets of phrases, match the beginning phrases with the correct ending phrases.

297. Answer four questions pertaining to the meaning of a

ITEM   INSTRUCTIONAL OBJECTIVE

The student is able to . . .

story in a basic reader.

298.   Given six simple sentences related to a story in a basic reader, identify correct and incorrect statements by marking *yes* or *no.*

299.   Recall details in a story read in a basic reader by correctly answering five out of six questions.

300.   Given three sentences from a story read, select the one that tells the main idea of the story.

301.   Given a question, locate and read a sentence in a basic reader that states the answer.

302.   Given four sentences that tell events in a story, number the sentences in sequential order.

303.   Use the table of contents to locate units and specific stories.

304.   Read a description and identify the thing described.

305.   After reading a story, summarize it.

306.   Demonstrate an understanding that the consonant "c" has no sound of its own but represents a "k" sound (hard c) or an "s" (soft c) by pronouncing the sound in words.

307.   Given a list of words with the consonant "c," write one column of words containing the "k" sound and one column containing the "s" sound.

308.   Given a list of words with the consonant "g," write one column of words containing the soft sound (j) and one column containing the hard sound (g).

309.   Identify that "q" is always found in combination with "u" and has the sound of "kw."

310.   Identify that the letter "x" has different sounds (eks in x ray, ks in box, gz in exit, and z in xylophone).

311.   When a root word ends in "y," change the "y" to "i" and add an ending.

312.   When a root word ends in "f," change the "f" to "v" before adding "es."

313.   Read hyphenated words.

ITEM INSTRUCTIONAL OBJECTIVE

The student is able to . . .

314. Demonstrate that phonic principles apply to vowels in accented syllables by stating the sound of the vowels in such words.

315. Identify the number of syllables (up to 3) in words presented orally.

316. Given a list of fifteen words from a basic word list, write the number of syllables beside each word.

317. Indicate which syllable is accented in a word presented orally.

318. Identify that the first syllable in words of two or three syllables is usually accented by marking the accent in such words.

319. Identify that the root part of a word is usually accented by marking the accent in such words.

320. Given a list of two syllable words, divide the words.

321. Alphabetize words by multiple initial letters (*aa*rduark, *ac*ademy).

322. Given ten words from a basic word list and ten sentences with blanks, write in the correct word for each sentence.

323. Given a list of ten words from a basic word list and ten brief definitions, match each word with the correct definition.

324. Given a list of ten sentences, with an underlined word in each and a list of ten definitions, read each sentence and match the underlined word with its definition.

325. Read six questions concerning a story in a basic reader and write the answers to the questions.

326. Given ten sentences from a story, read and identify a correct statement by marking *yes* and an incorrect statement by marking *no*.

327. Recall and relate details in a story read in a basic reader by correctly answering five out of six questions.

328. Indicate the main idea of a story by selecting from three titles the title most appropriate.

ITEM	INSTRUCTIONAL OBJECTIVE

The student is able to . . .

329.   Given ten sentences with blanks from a story from a basic reader, fill in the blank in each sentence with the correct information and indicate the page number where the word is found.

330.   Given five sentences from a basic reader telling the events in a story, number the sentences in sequential order.

331.   Read a paragraph and select the descriptive word that best tells how the character feels.

332.   Use the glossary to find the meaning of words.

333.   Read and follow written directions.

334.   Given ten sentences with blanks, choose between two words the word that will make the sentence true.

335.   Identify how characters in a story are different and alike.

336.   Mark the long, short, and silent vowels in words.

337.   Read contractions (I'm, I've, we'll, couldn't, didn't, can't) and tell the words the contractions were made from.

338.   Given the words *let us, cannot, do not,* and *did not,* write contractions using the words.

339.   Given the words *could not, we will, I have,* and *I am,* write contractions using the words.

340.   Given ten words from a word list and ten definitions, match the words with the definitions.

341.   Given a list of ten sentences with an italic word in each and a list of ten definitions, read each sentence and match the italic word with its definition.

342.   Given a word and two or three definitions, select the definition of the word as used in a sentence.

343.   Read ten questions about a story in a reader and write the answers to the questions.

344.   Locate the telephone number of a friend in the directory.

345.   Locate the telephone number of a business establish-

ITEM   INSTRUCTIONAL OBJECTIVE
_____

The student is able to . . .

        ment in the yellow pages of the directory.

346.   Use an encyclopedia to locate information about a person, a place, an event, and an object.

347.   Read TV, radio, and movie listings.

348.   Given a newspaper article, explain why the headline was used.

349.   Given newspaper editorials, state the authors' points of view and comment critically upon them.

350.   Given statements taken from advertisements, comment critically upon them.

_____

RESEARCH SKILLS

351.   Visit a library and pick out fiction books and nonfiction books.

352.   Visit a library and locate the card catalogue and explain how to use it.

353.   Given the terms *table of contents, glossary, index, appendix,* and *footnote,* define each and explain its purpose.

354.   Given a book, locate the table of contents and from it summarize the content of the book.

355.   Given a tour of the library, identify the reference books.

356.   Given a topic to research, itemize possible sources to use.

357.   Given a topic and a reference book, locate the topic in the book.

358.   Given an encyclopedia, define its purpose.

359.   Given a topic for research in the encyclopedia, locate it and summarize it in writing.

360.   Given a newspaper, list its various sections.

_____

ITEM	INSTRUCTIONAL OBJECTIVE

A SURVEY OF OCCUPATION-RELATED MATERIALS

The student is able to read, summarize in writing, develop a vocabulary and spelling list from, and discuss with the class the following:

361. An armed forces brochure.
362. A summary of the Child Labor Laws.
363. A description of new car models.
364. A driving manual.
365. A government brochure.
366. A hobby book.
367. A summary of an insurance policy.
368. A do-it-yourself manual.
369. A manual of instruction for an appliance.
370. An occupation description pamphlet.
371. A Social Security pamphlet.
372. A home safety check list.
373. A federal income tax manual.
374. A state income tax manual.
375. A travel folder.
376. A transportation schedule.
377. A vocational-technical school bulletin.
378. An advertisement brochure.
379. An autobiographical article.
380. An advertisement of a community event.
381. A code of behavior.
382. A cookbook.
383. The directions for assembling something.
384. The directions from a fire extinguisher.
385. A guide to a city.
386. A collection of greeting cards.
387. A home care pamphlet.
388. Magazine articles.
389. A mail-order catalogue.
390. A collection of proverbs.
391. A review of a movie.
392. A review of a television program.

ITEM   INSTRUCTIONAL OBJECTIVE

The student is able to read, summarize in writing, develop a vocabulary and spelling list from, and discuss with the class the following:

393. A review of a concert.
394. A scientific periodical.
395. An account of a sports event.
396. The general information section of the telephone directory.

VOCATIONAL LEARNING EXPERIENCES

Given the opportunity to do the following, the student will be able to locate information and read about it, summarize it in writing, develop a related vocabulary and spelling list from it, and discuss it with the class:

397. Clean a paint brush.
398. Cut molding.
399. Change a washer.
400. Hang a door.
401. Refinish furniture.
402. Read a blueprint.
403. Make a wooden box.
404. Use an electric drill.
405. Make an extension cord.
406. Make a campfire.
407. Set up a tent.
408. Take inventory.
409. Stock shelves.
410. Set up a display.
411. Read a road map.
412. Wash windows.
413. Arrange flowers.
414. Care for a plant.
415. Care for a lawn.
416. Weed a garden.
417. Wash and polish a car.

ITEM	INSTRUCTIONAL OBJECTIVE

Given the opportunity to do the following, the student will be able to locate information and read about it, summarize it in writing, develop a related vocabulary and spelling list from it, and discuss it with the class:

418. Change a tire.
419. Assemble a small motor.
420. Repair defective machinery.
421. Clean a spark plug.
422. Solder.
423. Read an electric meter.
424. Construct a walk.
425. Lay cement blocks.
426. Replace a windowpane.
427. Style hair.
428. Embroider a monogram.
429. Paint a wall.
430. Use a duplicating machine.
431. Use an adding machine.
432. Use a typewriter.
433. Use an electronic calculator.
434. Groom a dog.
435. Plant a tree.

Unit II

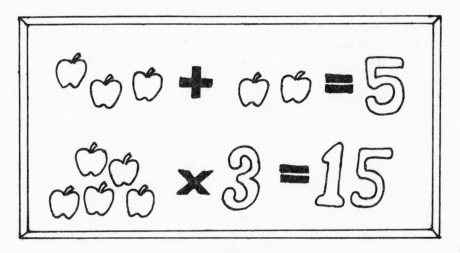

MATHEMATICS
SKILLS

THE developmental program for mathematics consists of three sections of instructional objectives: (1) numeration, (2) mathematical operations, and (3) measurement. In the last part of the program, the mathematics will be job-life oriented. For the special needs learner, who acquires the fundamentals of mathematics as presented developmentally, the program should also enable the knowledge to be put to use. For the student who has not yet acquired skill in the fundamentals, a practical program is the only effective motivation to continue developing skills. At this point the use of digital calculators may be desirable and indeed may be more effective.

Selected for the upper level are specific areas in which mathematics is involved. In each area there are problems which utilize each of the four basic functions — addition, subtraction, multiplication, and division — as well as combinations of them. For most areas, fractions, decimals, and percents, as well as whole numbers, may be used. The instructor, of course, will provide problems as practical and as varied as the topic permits.

In each area a learner will be faced with the situation of, first, determining the procedure to use and, second, utilizing skills previously learned. It is expected that this technique will prove most practical and will be of greatest long-range value.

INSTRUCTIONAL UNIT: NUMERATION

ITEM   INSTRUCTIONAL OBJECTIVE

The student is able to . . .
1. Demonstrate the concepts of 1,2,3,4, and 5 by matching structural materials.
2. Demonstrate the concepts of one-to-one correspondence by matching concrete objects.
3. Follow oral directions containing the words *one, one more,* and *another one.*
4. Count by rote from 1 to 5.
5. Count by rote from 1 to 10.
6. Count objects 1 to 5.
7. Select a given number of objects (1 through 5).
8. Count five objects in a line.
9. Copy the written symbols 1,2,3,4, and 5.
10. Write from dictation the written symbols 1 through 5.
11. Write the written symbols 1 through 5 in sequence when spoken.
12. Write the written symbols 1 through 5 when dictated in random order.
13. Count by rote from 1 to 30.
14. Count objects from 1 to 10.
15. Select a given number of objects (1 through 10) from a group.
16. Count ten objects in a line.
17. Recognize and name the written symbol 1.
18. Match "1" with a picture of one object.
19. Recognize and name the written symbol 2.
20. Match "2" with a picture of two objects.
21. Recognize and name the written symbol 3.
22. Match "3" with a picture of three objects.
23. Recognize and name the written symbol 4.
24. Match "4" with a picture of four objects.
25. Recognize and name the written symbol 5.
26. Match "5" with a picture of five objects.
27. Recognize and name the written symbol 6.

ITEM   INSTRUCTIONAL OBJECTIVE

The student is able to . . .

28. Match "6" with a picture of six objects.
29. Recognize and name the written symbol 7.
30. Match "7" with a picture of seven objects.
31. Recognize and name the written symbol 8.
32. Match "8" with a picture of eight objects.
33. Recognize and name the written symbol 9.
34. Match "9" with a picture of nine objects.
35. Recognize and name the written symbol 10.
36. Match "10" with a picture of ten objects.
37. Tell the number that comes after each number 1 through 10.
38. Tell the number that comes before each number 1 through 10.
39. Select the appropriate item when given ordinals (first through fifth).
40. Copy the numerals 1 through 10.
41. Write from dictation 1 through 10.
42. Write 1 through 10 independently in sequence.
43. Write independently 1 through 10 when dictated in random order.
44. Read the words for numbers 1 through 10 and match the word with the correct number of objects.
45. Verbalize that "0" means nothing or not any.
46. Begin understanding "odd" and "even" by contributing to a discussion that some things are bought singly and other things in pairs.
47. Name even and odd numbers 1 through 10.
48. Count by rote from 1 to 100.
49. Select a given number of objects from a group (1 through 30).
50. Count thirty objects in a line.
51. Recognize and name the written symbols 11,12,13,14, and 15.
52. Match the written symbols 11,12,13,14, and 15 with pictures showing the same number of objects.

ITEM   INSTRUCTIONAL OBJECTIVE

The student is able to . . .

53. Recognize and name the written symbols 16,17,18, and 19.
54. Match the written symbols 16,17,18, and 19 with pictures showing the same number of objects.
55. Recognize and name the written symbol 20.
56. Match the written symbol 20 with a picture showing twenty objects.
57. Recognize and name the written symbols 21,22,23,24, and 25.
58. Match the written symbols 21,22,23,24, and 25 with pictures showing the same number of objects.
59. Recognize and name the written symbols 26,27,28, and 29.
60. Match the written symbols 26,27,28, and 29 with pictures showing the same number of objects.
61. Recognize and name the written symbol 30.
62. Match the written symbol 30 with a picture of thirty objects.
63. Identify the ordinals first through tenth by selecting a given object in a line.
64. Tell the number that comes after each number 10 through 29.
65. Tell the number that comes before each number 12 through 30.
66. Copy the written symbols 0 through 100.
67. Write from dictation the written symbols 1 through 30.
68. Write the written symbols 1 through 30 in sequence.
69. Write the written symbols 1 through 30 when dictated in random order.
70. Write the words for numbers 1 through 10 and then match each word with its written symbol.
71. Read the ordinals first through tenth.
72. Understand place value by telling the number of tens and ones in the numbers 0 through 30.
73. Name the even and odd numbers 1 through 20.

ITEM	INSTRUCTIONAL OBJECTIVE

The student is able to . . .

74. Count 1 to 100.
75. Read and write the written symbols 1 through 100.
76. Recognize and name the written symbols 31 through 50.
77. Match the written symbols 31 through 50 with pictures showing the same number of objects.
78. Recognize and name the written symbols 51 through 100.
79. Match the written symbols 51 through 100 with pictures showing the same number of objects.
80. Arrange the numbers 1 through 100 on a number track.
81. Count and write by tens to 100.
82. Count and write by fives to 50.
83 Count and write by twos to 20, beginning with 2.
84 Count and write by twos to 19, beginning with 1.
85. Use the number line to add and subtract the numbers 1 through 100.
86. Fill in a number chart with the numbers 1 through 100.
87. Tell the number that comes before each number 30 through 50.
88. Tell the number that comes after each number 30 through 49.
89. Tell the number that comes before each number 50 through 100.
90. Tell the number that comes after each number 50 through 99.
91. Write from dictation the written symbols 1 through 100.
92. Write independently the written symbols 1 through 100 in sequence.
93. Write from memory the words for numbers 11 through 20.
94. Write from memory the ordinals first through tenth.
95. Divide the teen numbers into tens and ones using structural devices.
96. Divide the teen numbers into tens and ones without structural devices.

ITEM   INSTRUCTIONAL OBJECTIVE

The student is able to . . .

97. Demonstrate an understanding of place value by telling the number of tens and ones in the numbers 0 through 100.

98. Demonstrate an understanding that facts applying to units also apply to tens (3 + 4 = 7, 30 + 40 = 70).

99. Demonstrate an understanding that even numbers can be divided into two equal groups by dividing each even number from 2 to 20 into two equal groups.

100. Demonstrate an understanding that an odd number is an even number plus one.

101. Given any even number 2 through 18, tell the next even number.

102. Given any odd number 1 through 17, tell the next odd number.

103. Count from 1 to 500.

104. Read and write the written symbols 1 through 500.

105. Write the number of hundreds, tens, and ones in any number from 1 to 500.

106. Read and write the Roman numerals I,II,III,IV,V,VI, VII,VIII,IX,X,XI, and XII.

107. Count to 1000 by hundreds.

108. Write correctly the written symbol for a three- or four-place number.

109. Write correctly the written symbol for a three- or four-place number in a column showing thousands, hundreds, tens, and ones.

110. Read and write the words for numbers 10,20,30,40, 50,60,70,80,90, and 100.

111. Read and write the words for numbers 1 through 20.

112. Read the words for numbers up to 1000.

113. Read and write Roman numerals I through XX.

114. Read and write the written symbols for five-place numbers.

115. Read and write the words for numbers 1 through 100.

116. Write the written symbol for a five-place number when

ITEM INSTRUCTIONAL OBJECTIVE

The student is able to . . .
       it is given orally.
   117. Write a five-place number in columns showing ten
        thousands, thousands, hundreds, tens, and ones.

INSTRUCTIONAL UNIT: MATHEMATICAL OPERATIONS

ITEM	INSTRUCTIONAL OBJECTIVE

The student is able to . . .

1. Demonstrate the concept of equality and inequality by matching objects according to size and shape.
2. Match sets of objects (up to 5).
3. Demonstrate what happens when something is added or taken away from a group.
4. Cross out objects from a group to match a number shown (1 through 5).
5. Distinguish between pictures that show a whole and part of a number.
6. Demonstrate an understanding that addition is putting together by using concrete objects to discover addition facts.
7. Solve addition problems (up to 5) using concrete or structural materials.
8. Read a problem containing the plus (+) sign and solve correctly.
9. Demonstrate an understanding that subtraction is taking away by using concrete objects to discover subtraction facts.
10. Solve subtraction problems (up to 5) using concrete or structural materials.
11. Read a problem containing the minus (–) sign and solve correctly.
12. Solve a problem containing the word *add* when presented orally, using concrete objects.
13. Using concrete objects, solve an oral problem containing the words *find the sum.*
14. Using concrete objects, solve an oral problem containing the words *take away.*
15. Using concrete objects, solve an oral problem containing the words *find the difference.*
16. Identify drawings that show halves of a circle.
17. Color one-half and one-fourth of a circle.

ITEM	INSTRUCTIONAL OBJECTIVE

The student is able to . . .

18. Use a number line (0 through 10) to solve problems.
19. Supply the sums in addition facts 1 through 5.
20. Supply the sums in addition facts 6 through 10.
21. Using concrete objects, solve problems given orally that contain the words *add to, plus,* and *total.*
22. Solve an addition problem with two digits having a sum no more than 10.
23. Solve an addition problem with three digits having a sum no more than 10.
24. Solve addition problems with digits of zero.
25. Supply the remainder in the subtraction facts using digits through 10.
26. Using concrete objects, solve problems given orally that contain the words *subtract, minus, take away,* and *from.*
27. Solve addition problems written in equation form $(1 + 1 = , 2 + 1 =)$.
28. Solve subtraction problems written in equation form $(1 - 1 = , 2 - 1 =)$.
29. Given any addition fact (through 10), write the related subtraction fact $(3 + 2 = , 3 - 2 =)$.
30. Given any subtraction fact (through 10), write the related addition fact $(3 - 2 = , 3 + 2 =)$.
31. Give two groups of objects whose sum is less than 10 and write the related addition and subtraction facts.
32. Use a number line to add and subtract numbers 1 through 10 (0 1 2③4⑤6 7 8 9 10; 0 1 2③4⑤6 7 8 9 10).
33. Recognize and add the doubles (through 5) $(2 + 2 = , 5 + 5 =)$.
34. Know the addition facts for doubles by stating the sum when the digits are presented.
35. Recognize and identify equal groups (⊂⊃ . . . ⊂⊃).
36. Given eight objects grouped in twos, form two groups of four objects (⊂ . . ⊃ ⊂ . . ⊃).
37. Given six objects grouped in threes, form three groups of two objects.

ITEM   INSTRUCTIONAL OBJECTIVE

The student is able to . . .

38. Group objects in twos, fives, and tens.
39. Verbalize the process used to find one-half of a group in division.
40. Solve simple addition word problems.
41. Solve simple subtraction word problems.
42. Demonstrate understanding of the forty-five easy addition facts by stating the sums presented on flash cards.
43. Solve addition problems involving one-place numbers to three digits having a sum no more than 10 (3 + 1 + 2 = 6).
44. Check addition problems by adding in the opposite direction.
45. Add units to a two-place number in a problem that does not require regrouping.
46. Add two two-place numbers in a problem that does not require regrouping.
47. Work addition problems that involve adding 10 to a two-place number.
48. Work addition problems that involve adding several tens to a two-place number.
49. Work addition problems that require transfer of tens in higher decades without regrouping (5 + 5 = 10, 15 + 5 = 20).
50. Demonstrate understanding of the subtraction facts with digits through 9, when the problems are presented on flash cards.
51. Supply the remainders in subtraction facts with digits exceeding 10.
52. Work subtraction problems involving units from a two-place number without regrouping.
53. Work subtraction problems involving subtracting 10 from a two-place number.
54. Work subtraction problems that require the transfer of tens from higher decades without regrouping (10 − 4 = 6, 30 − 4 = 26).

ITEM	INSTRUCTIONAL OBJECTIVE

The student is able to . . .

55. Check subtraction problems by adding.
56. Recognize and add the doubles 6 through 10.
57. Read a problem containing the multiplication (·) sign and solve the problem.
58. Demonstrate an understanding of multiplication facts for 2 (2×2 through 2×12) by stating the product when the factors are presented on flash cards.
59. Demonstrate an understanding of reverses for the multiplication facts for 2 when the factors are presented on flash cards.
60. Demonstrate an understanding of multiplication facts for 3 (3×2 through 3×12) when the factors are presented on flash cards.
61. Analyze the numbers 1 through 10 by combining, separating, and rearranging objects and recording the addition and subtraction facts represented ($4; 3 + 1 = 4, 1 + 3 = 4, 4 \quad 1 = 3, 4 - 3 = 1, 2 + 2 = 4, 4 - 2 = 2$).
62. Analyze the numbers 11 through 20 by combining, separating, and rearranging objects and recording the addition and subtraction facts represented ($12; 6 + 6 = 12, 12 - 6 = 6, 7 + 5 = 12, 5 + 7 = 12, 12 - 7 = 5, 12 - 5 = 7, 8 + 4 = 12$, etc.).
63. Solve addition problems with two-place digits that do not involve regrouping ($30 + 10 + 20 = 60$).
64. Add two-place numbers with three-place sums in a problem that does not involve regrouping.
65. Add even hundreds.
66. Add 3 two- or three-place numbers with three-place sums that involve regrouping in one or two places.
67. Solve addition problems with five digits.
68. Add one-, two-, and three-place numbers with internal zeros.
69. Know the subtraction facts with digits exceeding ten by stating the remainders when presented on flash cards.
70. Solve subtraction problems that involve two- and three-

ITEM   INSTRUCTIONAL OBJECTIVE

The student is able to . . .
  place numbers that do not require regrouping.
71. Solve subtraction problems that involve regrouping.
72. Subtract two- and three-place numbers, regrouping tens and ones.
73. Subtract two- and three-place numbers, regrouping hundreds and tens.
74. Subtract two- and three-place numbers, regrouping hundreds, tens, and ones.
75. Subtract two- and three-place numbers with internal zeros, regrouping in all places.
76. Divide numbers (50 or less) into equal parts.
77. Know the multiplication facts for fours by stating the product (4 × 2 through 4 × 12).
78. Know the multiplication facts for fives by stating the product.
79. Multiply two- and three-place numbers by a one-place number without regrouping.
80. Multiply two- and three-place numbers with zeros by a one-place number without regrouping.
81. Know the division facts with divisors of 2 by stating the quotient when the divisors and dividends are presented on flash cards.
82. Know the division facts with divisors of 3 by stating the quotient when the divisors and dividends are presented on flash cards.
83. Know the division facts with divisors of 4 by stating the quotient when the divisors and dividends are presented on flash cards.
84. Know the division facts with divisors of 5 by stating the quotient when the divisors and dividends are presented on flash cards.
85. Know the division facts with divisors of 0 by stating the quotient when the divisors and dividends are presented on flash cards.
86. Know the division facts with divisors of 1 by stating the

ITEM   INSTRUCTIONAL OBJECTIVE
_____

The student is able to . . .

quotient when the divisors and dividends are presented on flash cards.

87. Divide both short division and equation forms.

88. Divide two- and three-place dividends by one-place divisors.

89. Divide problems that have 0 in the dividend.

90. Divide problems that have 0's and 1's in the quotient.

91. Check a multiplication fact by dividing.

92. Given any multiplication fact (through 5), write the related division fact.

93. Given any division fact (through 5), write the related multiplication fact.

94. Solve word problems that require the addition and subtraction of two-place numbers without regrouping.

95. Solve one-step word problems that involve addition, subtraction, multiplication, and division.

96. Add three-place numbers, regrouping in all places.

97. Add four-place numbers, regrouping in all places.

98. Solve addition problems with 7 one-place digits.

99. Add 5 two- or three-place numbers, regrouping in all places.

100. Add 6 two- and three-place numbers, regrouping in all places.

101. Add 5 four-place numbers.

102. Check addition problems by subtraction.

103. Solve three-place subtraction problems, regrouping in all places.

104- State products of multiplication facts for 6,7,8,9,10,11,
110. and 12 when factors are presented on flash cards.

111. Solve problems using the long form of multiplication.

112. Multiply a two-place number by a one-place number in a problem that requires regrouping.

113. Multiply a three-place number by a one-place number

ITEM   INSTRUCTIONAL OBJECTIVE

The student is able to . . .

in a problem that requires regrouping in all places.

114. Check a multiplication problem by reversing the factors and multiplying.

115- Know the division facts with divisors of 6,7,8, and 9 by
119. stating the quotient correctly when the divisors and dividends are presented on flash cards.

120. Divide a number by a one-place number with or without a remainder.

121. Divide a three-place number by a one-place number using the short form of division.

122. Divide a three-place number by a one-place number using the long form of division.

123. Divide a four-place number by a one-place number using the short form of division.

124. Divide a four-place number by a one-place number using the long form of division.

125. Work a division problem with a one-place divisor and a two-place quotient.

126. Add fractional numbers with sums less than 1 that have the same denominator.

127. Understand 1 1/2 by drawing a picture showing the amount of one and one-half.

128. Understand 1 1/3, 1 2/3, 1 1/4, and 1 3/4 by shading drawings to represent the amounts.

129. Take a recipe, divide the amounts in half, and record the new quantities needed.

130. Take a recipe, double the amounts, and record the new quantities needed.

131. Find 50 percent of a given even number.

132. Find a given percent of any number when the problem involves whole numbers.

133. Add seven-place numbers, regrouping in all places.

134. Multiply numbers by 10 and 100 by adding zeros.

135. Multiply four-place numbers using zero in different places.

ITEM   INSTRUCTIONAL OBJECTIVE
_____

The student is able to . . .
136. Divide numbers by 10 and by 100 by moving the decimal point.
137. Read, write, add, and subtract fractions up to and including eighths.
138. Read and write decimals to hundredths.
139. Work problems in decimal form.
140. Compute interest rates.

INSTRUCTIONAL UNIT: MEASUREMENT

ITEM	INSTRUCTIONAL OBJECTIVE

The student is able to . . .

1. Verbalize the concept that money is used to buy goods.
2. Verbalize three ways that people earn money.
3. Identify by name a *penny,* a *nickel,* and a *dime.*
4. Describe day and night.
5. Compare objects according to weight.
6. Name items that can be bought with a penny, those with a nickel, and those with a dime.
7. Match coins of equal value (5 pennies equals 1 nickel).
8. Follow oral instructions containing the words *before* and *after.*
9. Name activities that take place during the morning, noon, afternoon, and evening.
10. State the purpose of a clock.
11. Identify a calendar and its purpose.
12. Accurately state his age.
13. Select between short and long lengths of ribbon.
14. Select between stacks of blocks the stack that is short and the stack that is tall.
15. Differentiate between heavy and light objects.
16. Select from a group of objects the one that is heaviest and the one that is lightest.
17. Name objects that are hot and objects that are cold.
18. Correctly designate containers of water that are warm and those that are cool.
19. Differentiate between containers measuring a cup and those measuring a pint.
20. Identify and name a quarter, a half-dollar, and a dollar bill.
21. Verbalize events related to today, yesterday, and tomorrow.
22. Use *early, on time,* and *late* in correct response to questions asked.
23. Read the numbers on a clock.

ITEM	INSTRUCTIONAL OBJECTIVE

The student is able to . . .

24. Name the days of the week.
25. Name the days of the week in sequence.
26. Verbalize several of the differences in the four seasons.
27. State his birth date.
28. Identify inch and foot on a ruler.
29. Identify a pint container and a quart container.
30. Relate the temperature to the weather by verbalizing the day as hot, cold, cool, or warm.
31. State the value of a quarter, half-dollar, and one dollar bill.
32. Solve problems given orally to find total cost, how much money is left, and how much money is needed.
33. Make change from a nickel and from a dime.
34. State the value of any combination of coins with amounts totaling $.30 or less.
35. Identify the long hands and the short hands on a clock and tell the function of each.
36. State the meaning of AM as the time between midnight and noon.
37. State the meaning of PM as the time between noon and midnight.
38. Tell time using the terms *quarter past, 15 minutes after, quarter after,* and *quarter of.*
39. Tell time at hour and half-hour intervals.
40. Tell time on the half-hour by using the expressions *thirty, half-past,* and *thirty minutes past.*
41. Pronounce the names of the months.
42. Read the names of the month on a calendar.
43. Tell the number of months in a year.
44. Locate important holidays on a calendar.
45. Understand leap year by verbalizing the concept.
46. Locate the present date on a calendar.
47. Locate his birthday on the calendar.
48. Distinguish between a foot ruler and a yardstick.
49. Recognize the word *yard* and state its meaning.

ITEM INSTRUCTIONAL OBJECTIVE

The student is able to . . .

50. Differentiate between containers that measure a quart and those that measure a gallon.
51. Demonstrate the understanding that money can purchase goods and services by stating things that can be obtained for money.
52. Recognize and use the dollar ($) and cent (¢) signs.
53. Make change for $1.00.
54. Relate dollars, dimes, and cents to hundreds, tens, and ones working a problem with money.
55. Work a problem that involves adding and subtracting dimes from a dollar ($1.00 − .70 = .30).
56. Record-time by the hour and the half-hour.
57. Name the months of the year in sequence.
58. Record his birth date using numbers (3/24/60).
59. State the dates of important holidays.
60. Using a ruler, draw a line one inch long and a line one foot long.
61. Read the words inch and foot and demonstrate their meaning.
62. Identify the abbreviations *in.* and *ft.*
63. Relate how we measure pounds by naming things measured in pounds.
64. State the number of ounces in a pound.
65. Identify ounce, cup, pint, quart, half-gallon, and gallon containers.
66. Read a weather thermometer correctly.
67. Read and write the amounts of money using the cent (¢) sign for 1¢ to 99¢.
68. Read and write amounts of money in decimal form ($.01 to $10.00).
69. Multiply money in decimal form.
70. Divide money in decimal form.
71. Verbalize: 1 hour equals 60 minutes.
72. State time to the minute and read time to the minute.
73. Set the time and alarm signal on a clock.

ITEM	INSTRUCTIONAL OBJECTIVE

The student is able to . . .

74. Estimate lengths, measure lengths, and compare the estimate with the measure.
75. Measure the classroom floor area.
76. Work a problem involving equivalent measures: 1 yard equals 3 feet or 36 inches.
77. Measure lengths that include 1/2 and 1/4 inch.
78. Indicate a place that is 1 mile away from the school.
79. Read measures of distances as shown on road maps.
80. Read and write the abbreviations for pound (lb.) and ounce (oz.).
81. Read a scale and determine weights that include 1/2 and 1/4 pounds.
82. Read and write abbreviations for cup, pint, quart, and gallon.
83. Tell the equivalent measures of gallon, 1/2 gallon, quart, pint, 1/2 pint, and cup.
84. Solve a problem based on equivalent liquid measurements.
85. Contribute to a class discussion about the temperature needed to refrigerate, freeze, and cook food.
86. Count and make change using coins and bills in any denomination.
87. Weigh letters, determine the amount of postage, and purchase stamps to mail the letters.
88. Make out a budget that includes savings and tell why savings are important.
89. Explain the services offered by a bank.
90. Explain a checking account.
91. Explain a savings account.
92. Explain bank loans.
93. Discuss several ways money is earned.
94. Understand and verbalize that there are 60 seconds in a minute.
95. Solve problems that require adding minutes and change minutes to hours and minutes.

ITEM   INSTRUCTIONAL OBJECTIVE

The student is able to . . .

96. Solve problems that require adding seconds and change seconds to minutes and seconds.
97. Read and explain size markers in clothing.
98. Measure using a tape and folding ruler.
99. Read an odometer.
100. Compute distances between cities.
101. Read a scale and determine weights that include fractions of a pound.
102. State that there are 16 ounces in a pound.
103. Solve problems based on equivalent measures of weight.
104. Identify a bushel and name items sold by the bushel.
105. Measure quantities using a teaspoon, tablespoon, fractions of a cup, and a cup.
106. Read and write abbreviations for teaspoon (tsp.) and tablespoon (tblsp.).
107. Understand Fahrenheit and Centigrade scales by reading thermometers and oven temperature gauges.
108. Add the costs of purchases and make change.
109. State the difference between a savings account and a checking account.

INSTRUCTIONAL UNIT: LIFE-ORIENTED MATHEMATICS

ITEM	INSTRUCTIONAL OBJECTIVE

(Arithmetic problems for higher skill learners should include addition, subtraction, multiplication, and division involving whole numbers, decimals, fractions, and percents wherever applicable to the specified topic.)

Given an arithmetic problem related to the following topics, the student will select the proper mathematical process and compute the solution:

1. Sales advertisements.
2. Buying groceries.
3. Calendars.
4. Road signs.
5. Road maps.
6. Transportation schedules.
7. Recipes.
8. Thermometers.
9. Clocks.
10. Time zones.
11. Mileage.
12. Currency.
13. Sales slips.
14. Checking accounts.
15. Gross wages.
16. Net wages.
17. Savings accounts.
18. Budget.
19. Telephone bills.
20. Electric bills.
21. Batting averages.
22. Expense accounts.
23. Charge accounts.
24. Scale drawings.
25. Directional compass.
26. Digital calculators.
27. Rifle trajectory.
28. Land measurement.

ITEM   INSTRUCTIONAL OBJECTIVE
_____

Given an arithmetic problem related to the following topics, the student will select the proper mathematical process and compute the solution:

29. Operation of a vehicle.
30. Financing.
31. Shopping for clothes.
32. Coupons.
33. Renting a house.
34. Mortgages.
35. Utilities.
36. Time measurements.
37. Statistical graphs.
38. Discounts.
39. Fund raising projects.
40. Working overtime.
41. Buying dressmaking material.
42. Installment buying.
43. Sales tax.
44. Weighing vegetables.
45. Building construction.
46. Sewing.
47. Social Security.
48. Unit pricing.
49. Measuring angles.
50. Credit cards.
51. Savings bonds.
52. Income tax.
53. Property tax.
54. Wage tax.
55. Wage deductions.
56. Life insurance.
57. Automobile insurance.
58. Liability insurance.
59. Fire insurance.
60. Health and accident insurance.
61. Retirement insurance.

Unit III

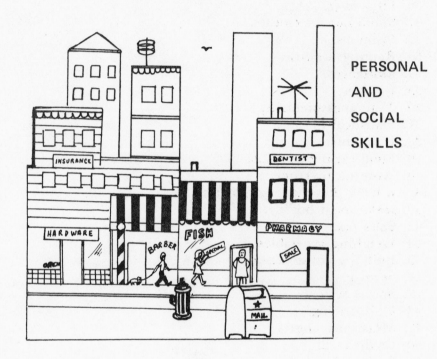

PERSONAL

AND

SOCIAL

SKILLS

HUMAN
ECOLOGY:
PERSONAL

THE special needs learner should learn the fundamentals of health care during the early school years. Therefore, the last part of the health program emphasizes an understanding of the reasons for personal health care and prepares the learner for serious health-related concerns and problems.

The human ecology program on health focuses on the development of basic hygiene and personal health care with particular emphasis on the adolescent. The program provides a general understanding of the systems of the body so that the student will have a frame of reference for understanding illnesses and accidents in later life.

The program on safety was included as a result of consideration of the very large number of accidents that occur in daily life. It is recommended that a Red Cross course in first aid eventually be made a part of the curriculum. Meanwhile, achievement of the objectives listed will provide the student with sufficient basic skills to assist himself or others in an accident.

Another widely recognized problem in American life is the widespread use of drugs and alcohol. Although not specifically included, the teacher may wish to develop student awareness of the dangers involved in the use of tobacco, alcohol, narcotics, and even medicines.

INSTRUCTIONAL UNIT: HEALTH AND SAFETY

ITEM   INSTRUCTIONAL OBJECTIVE

HEALTH

The student is able to . . .

1. Given a drawing of a person, name the body parts.
2. Given an incomplete drawing of a person, add the missing parts.
3. Given the command "Touch your _____ (eye, ear, nose, mouth, hair, arm, leg)," correctly identify each.
4. Given the description of a body function, identify the body part that performs that function.
5. Given the command "Touch your _____ (right or left foot, etc.)," perform the task and identify the correct body part.
6. Given a description of an individual (hair, eyes, height, weight, etc.), identify the person described.
7. Looking in a full length mirror, accurately describe himself.
8. Given a box with distinctive textures and shapes, identify the objects by touch.
9. Given pictures of selected seasons of the year, state the associated weather with the season.
10. Select the proper clothing for a designated season and/or activity from pictures presented.
11. Match pictures of mothers and their young (people, pets, wild animals, etc.).
12. State four ways mothers care for their young.
13. Compare personal abilities with an infant's by listing differences.
14. Demonstrate how to wash hands and face and clean nails.
15. Given pictures of foods, sort into categories of meats, fruits, and vegetables.
16. List foods eaten for breakfast, lunch, and dinner.
17. Make a picture display of foods, identifying the importance of a balanced diet for good health.
18. Discuss the importance of resting, including when

ITEM	INSTRUCTIONAL OBJECTIVE

The student is able to . . .

and how to rest after a strenuous activity (keep a record for a week of the number of hours of sleep).

19. Use the correct procedure in brushing teeth. (Use a model of teeth and ask the school nurse, if available, to demonstrate the procedure.)
20. List good health habits.
21. List symptoms of illness.
22. Demonstrate the procedure for washing raw foods.
23. List items required for personal cleanliness.
24. Given a weather prediction from the newspaper (cold, warm, rain, snow), indicate the appropriate clothing to wear.
25. Relate how germs enter and affect our bodies.
26. List precautions to take and procedures to follow when symptoms of illness appear.
27. Plan a balanced menu for a day.
28. List the parts of the ear.
29. Relate how the parts of the ear function.
30. List ways to protect the ear.
31. List the parts of the eye.
32. Discuss ways of protecting the eye.
33. List the major organs of the body.
34. Discuss the functions of the major body organs.
35. Demonstrate examples of good and poor posture.
36. Identify pests that can contaminate food.
37. Identify ways of preserving and protecting foods.
38. List ways of obtaining help when ill or in an accident (informing parents, teacher, and nurse and calling for a doctor or an ambulance).
39. List and discuss common diseases and their prevention.
40. Identify the health and first aid items needed in the home.
41. Discuss health conditions that can handicap an individual.
42. List factors necessary for maintaining a healthy body.

ITEM	INSTRUCTIONAL OBJECTIVE

The student is able to . . .

43. List factors necessary for maintaining good mental health.
44. Discuss the need for exercise and list several types.
45. List recommended daily steps for personal grooming.
46. List practices necessary to maintain healthy teeth.
47. List rules for care of the eyes and ears.
48. After a discussion of illnesses, list symptoms of the onset of sickness and recommend steps to be taken.
49. After a discussion of the circulatory system, list its parts and describe its functions.
50. After a discussion of the digestive system, list its parts and describe its functions.
51. After a discussion of the respiratory system, list its parts and describe its functions.
52. After a discussion of the skeletal system, point out the main bones of the body and their functions.
53. After discussing the nervous system, list the main parts and their functions.
54. After a discussion of the main muscles of the body, describe their functions.

SAFETY

1. Discuss the need for practicing safety rules in the home and school.
2. Identify the colored lights on a traffic signal.
3. Verbalize the meanings associated with the colors of a traffic light (red = stop).
4. List the rules of safe street crossing.
5. Discuss the need for practicing safety rules in motor vehicles.
6. Follow procedures used in a fire drill.
7. After a presentation or visit to a fire station, discuss the role of a fireman and procedures for reporting a fire.
8. After a discussion on hazards in the home, formulate a

ITEM	INSTRUCTIONAL OBJECTIVE

The student is able to . . .

list of safety rules.

9. Role-play the procedures followed both if he were awake and if he were sleeping when a fire occurred at home.

10. Given a list of animals, identify harmless animals from dangerous animals.

11. After a discussion on playground safety, demonstrate the safe use of playground equipment.

12. Discuss the dangers of going into an abandoned building, visiting construction sites, or playing inside abandoned equipment or appliances (freezer/refrigerator).

13. List the safety procedures to follow when riding a bicycle.

14. Identify safety signs.

15. Identify ways of preventing accidents within the community.

16. Role-play the procedures to be followed in getting help in an emergency.

17. Discuss the importance of locking automobile doors when traveling.

18. Given a discussion of recreation-related accidents, list safety rules for hunting, swimming, boating, etc.

19. Identify the safety procedures followed when using lawn/garden and other tools and equipment.

20. After a discussion of automobile fatalities, list causes of highway accidents.

21. After a discussion of safety in the home, list some causes of home accidents.

22. Demonstrate procedures to follow in case of bleeding and give proper first aid.

23. Demonstrate procedures to follow in case of choking and give proper first aid.

24. Demonstrate procedures to follow in case of shock and give proper first aid.

25. Demonstrate procedures to follow in case of an emer-

ITEM   INSTRUCTIONAL OBJECTIVE

The student is able to . . .

gency where artificial respiration is needed (heart attack, drowning) and give proper first aid.

26. Demonstrate procedures to follow in case of both mild and severe burns and give proper first aid.

27. Demonstrate procedures to follow in case of poisoning and give proper first aid.

28. Demonstrate procedures to follow in case of an animal bite and give proper first aid.

29. Demonstrate procedures to follow in case of broken bone and give proper first aid.

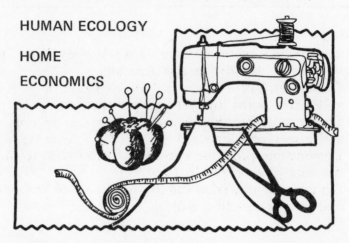

HUMAN ECOLOGY

HOME

ECONOMICS

The program in home economics was designed to provide both boys and girls with the basic information and skills necessary to be an effective household member.

The program includes sections on foods, clothing, child care, and common household emergencies. Each unit is composed of instructional objectives that almost everyone will eventually use. It is expected that each learner will be given the opportunity, at least once, of fulfilling each objective.

Those students with special interest and aptitude will spend more time in some areas and will explore vocational opportunities in the field, with teacher assistance. However, the course is essentially a practical one in which the student learns by doing. Attendant upon such a program is the expectation that the students will make mistakes. Making mistakes and rectifying them are inherent ingredients in such a course, and it is most important that the teacher encourage this understanding.

It is hoped that through the development of a "try it" attitude and the achievement of the listed objectives, the learner will take a very large step toward becoming a contributing and effective family member.

INSTRUCTIONAL UNIT: HOME ECONOMICS

ITEM	INSTRUCTIONAL OBJECTIVE

FOODS

The student is able to . . .

1. After an introductory discussion of home economics, list the general aims of the program.
2. After a tour of the home economics room, sketch the floor plan.
3. Develop a list of home economics related words by recording them in a notebook.
4. After a demonstration on the use of a stove, select the desired heat for the burners and the oven.
5. After a demonstration, clean a stove.
6. Prepare foods for refrigeration.
7. Following a demonstration in washing dishes by hand, scrape, rinse, and stack the dishes.
8. Given the correct order for washing dishes, wash silverware, glassware, china, and pots.
9. Given a stack of washed dishes, dry and place them in the proper storage area.
10. Prepare kitchen cabinets for use.
11. After instruction in the use of electric kitchen appliances (mixer, blender, toaster, can opener, knife, etc.), identify them and use them properly and safely.
12. Given utensils used in the kitchen and dining room (spoon, spatula, butter knife, etc.), use them properly.
13. After a demonstration, set the table for a meal.
14. Given instructions in table manners, employ them.
15. After a discussion of the body's need for food, list food groups to be included in each meal.
16. After a discussion of the "basic four" food groups, list and give specific examples of foods in each group.
17. After a discussion on the need for breakfast, prepare five breakfast menus.
18. Given a box of cold cereal, prepare a breakfast including it.

ITEM	INSTRUCTIONAL OBJECTIVE

The student is able to . . .

19. Given a box of hot cereal, prepare and serve it.
20. Given eggs, prepare them in three ways.
21. Given a recipe for hotcakes, waffles, or French toast, prepare and serve each.
22. Given situations in which lunches must be prepared, make up appropriate menus.
23. Given the ingredients, make a salad.
24. After a demonstration, make three kinds of soup.
25. Given luncheon menus, select, plan, and prepare five lunches.
26. Given leftovers from a dinner meal, use them to prepare a lunch.
27. Given the opportunity to purchase food for a meal, price the items in several stores to determine the best place to buy.
28. Given a dinner menu, make up a shopping list and purchase the items necessary for the preparation of the meal.
29. Broil a steak.
30. Roast a pork roast.
31. Fry fish.
32. Deep-fry a prepared chicken.
33. Prepare vegetables for serving.
34. Prepare potatoes in four different ways.
35. Given the ingredients, prepare a stew.
36. Given the recipe, prepare a casserole.
37. Prepare and cook fresh vegetables.
38. Given the recipes, make a pie, a cake, and a pudding.
39. After a discussion on the informal ways of serving a meal, distinguish between buffet and family style.
40. Given a dinner menu for a special occasion, purchase, prepare, and serve a five course dinner.
41. Given hypothetical situations in which lunches or dinners must be prepared with short notice, choose commercially prepared foods to serve.
42. After a discussion on special holiday meals, list several

ITEM   INSTRUCTIONAL OBJECTIVE

The student is able to . . .
    traditional holiday foods.
43. Prepare jelly or jam from fresh fruit.
44. Prepare several fresh vegetables and fruits for freezing.
45. Prepare several fresh vegetables and fruits for canning.
46. Given a specific amount of money with which to purchase a week's supply of food, list foods that would be bought.
47. Choose a dinner from a menu and then eat it in a restaurant.
48. Given a checklist, indicate which of the basic four food groups were included in selected meals.

CLOTHING
The student is able to . . .
1. Following a discussion on personal grooming, state characteristics of a well groomed person.
2. Shown photographs of persons dressed in various ways, match them with specific occasions.
3. Given several items of clothing, select a color-coordinated wardrobe for a given occasion.
4. Develop in a notebook a list of terms related to clothing and sewing.
5. Given clothing advertisements, compare clothing prices and quality of goods from information in the advertisements.
6. Explain the terms used on clothing labels.
7. Given a specific garment, estimate the cost if purchased and the cost if made at home.
8. Identify the fabrics of several articles of clothing.
9. Identify a spool of thread by number and purpose.
10. List the contents of a sewing box.
11. Mend a torn article of clothing.
12. Darn socks having holes.
13. State safety precautions when using a sewing machine.

ITEM	INSTRUCTIONAL OBJECTIVE

The student is able to . . .

14. Use a sewing machine to hem a skirt or pants.
15. Use a sewing machine to make buttonholes.
16. Take body measurements using a tape measure.
17. Determine size, width, and yardage of material required in using a pattern.
18. Choose a suitable fabric for a pattern.
19. Transfer a pattern to a fabric.
20. Cut out a pattern on a fabric.
21. Cut a fabric according to a pattern and then assemble it.
22. After a demonstration, make pleats.
23. Given hooks, eyes, snaps, and buttons, attach them to a fabric.
24. Sew a zipper into an article of clothing.
25. After receiving information about commercial laundering and home laundering, make a comparison of costs.
26. Given different fabrics, state correct laundering procedures.
27. Explain the purpose and use of various soaps, water softeners, bleaches, etc.
28. Compare several soaps and detergents as to price, purpose, and effectiveness.
29. Sort and then wash clothing in a washing machine.
30. Select the proper procedure for removing different types of stains from clothing.
31. List cautions to observe when using a clothes washer and dryer.
32. Discuss the purpose of the various settings and operate a clothes dryer correctly.
33. Discuss the various temperature settings on an electric iron.
34. Press a pair of slacks.
35. Properly hang various articles of clothing.
36. Store various articles of clothing safely from moths.

ITEM   INSTRUCTIONAL OBJECTIVE

CHILD CARE
The student is able to . . .
1. After a discussion on the impending arrival of an infant, list changes that will occur in the family.
2. Given a situation in which a gift must be chosen for a new baby, list appropriate gift suggestions.
3. Pick out furnishings for a new baby's room from a catalogue.
4. After a discussion on proper clothing, choose an infant's wardrobe relative to a given season.
5. Given a situation in which an infant is crying, suggest possible reasons and remedies.
6. After a demonstration, show how to dress a baby.
7. Given baby formulas of different kinds, prepare them correctly.
8. Prepare breakfast, lunch, and dinner for an infant, using commercially prepared baby food.
9. After a demonstration, show how to change a diaper.
10. Following a demonstration, show how to bathe an infant.
11. After a discussion regarding the physical well-being of a baby, list medical services needed.
12. Select toys for children of various ages from a toy catalogue.
13. Describe the steps to follow in putting children to bed.
14. After a discussion on the activities of toddlers, describe their characteristics.
15. Following a discussion on the behavior of small children, list reasons for crying, laughter, and fatigue.
16. Identify possible hazards to a toddler in the home.
17. Discuss the advantages and disadvantages of various disciplinary techniques in given situations.
18. Given situations in which a child exhibits fear, suggest possible causes and remedies.
19. Organize a play activity for several pre-school children.

ITEM   INSTRUCTIONAL OBJECTIVE

The student is able to . . .

20. Plan a menu, purchase the food, and prepare the meal for several young children.
21. List information that should be available in case of an emergency while baby-sitting.
22. Entertain a young child for an hour.

HOUSEHOLD EMERGENCIES

The student is able to . . .

1. After a demonstration, open a clogged drain.
2. Shut off the water and obtain help when a water leak occurs.
3. Given a situation in which an object is lost down a drain, remove the sink trap to retrieve it.
4. Suggest remedies for a continually running toilet.
5. After a discussion of emergency electrical situations, shut off the main electrical supply.
6. Following a discussion of home lighting malfunctions, replace the fuse.
7. After a demonstration, replace a broken light switch.
8. Suggest possible reasons that would cause an electrical appliance not to work.
9. Suggest causes and remedies in a situation where a furnace is inoperable.
10. List precautions to take during an electrical storm.
11. List safety precautions to take during a hurricane.
12. List precautions to take during a severe winter snowstorm.
13. After a discussion of fire occurring in a house, list safety procedures to follow.
14. Following a discussion of emergencies in the home, list emergency items that should be immediately available.

SOCIAL

SKILLS

The social skills program starts with social beginnings, covers the local and state community, expands to the national community, and broadens to the world community. Each unit presents objectives on the past, the environment, the government, and current problems. The instructional objectives also touch upon most social science areas — history, geography, civics, economics, sociology, and anthropology — as well as on the fundamental social skills of interpreting materials, critical thinking, and problem solving.

Each program is comprised of more than thirty instructional objectives — approximately one objective for each week of the school year or as desired by the instructor. It is strongly suggested that each instructional objective listed be broken down into several more specific objectives, daily lesson plans, or learning experiences. Materials and methodology will be determined by the special needs of the learner.

INSTRUCTIONAL UNIT: SOCIAL SKILLS

ITEM   INSTRUCTIONAL OBJECTIVE

SOCIAL BEGINNINGS

The student is able to . . .

1. Discuss his role in the family.
2. Discuss reasons for having a home.
3. List the similarities and differences of home life in the city and in the country.
4. Identify the location and function of various parts of the physical plant of the school (principal's office, janitorial service, nurses's room, rest room, cafeteria, gym, classroom, etc.).
5. Identify the location and function of various facilities in the neighborhood (churches, grocery stores, fire station, etc.).
6. List the similarities and differences of earning a living in the city and in the country.
7. Given a list of animals, identify those found in the country and/or the city.
8. Identify plants and animals found in the neighborhood.
9. Discuss the basic needs of animals and plants.
10. Discuss reasons why some people live in the city and some in the country.
11. Identify and discuss various modes of transportation and communication.
12. After a discussion on local, city, and county government, relate the functions of each.
13. Discuss local natural resources and ways of conserving them.
14. Relate the historical background of the community.
15. After a discussion on state and national government, relate the functions of each.
16. List and discuss the reasons for laws and their importance.

ITEM   INSTRUCTIONAL OBJECTIVE

LOCAL AND STATE COMMUNITY
The student is able to . . .
1. Given readings in aboriginal history, describe the life of the Indians of the local area.
2. After a discussion on the early settlers of the area, list some problems they faced and some of their solutions.
3. Given a biographical study of several prominent early Pennsylvanians (substitute his own state), explain the contributions of four of them.
4. After identifying early hand tools of Pennsylvania (his state), explain how they have been replaced by modern machinery.
5. After receiving instruction on the growth of agriculture in Pennsylvania (his state), explain how subsistance farming was replaced by the modern agricultural complex.
6. After receiving instruction on transportation and communication in early Pennsylvania (his state), relate how improvements aided the growth of the state.
7. After studying various cultural groups of Pennsylvania (his state), list the contributions of each.
8. After a discussion on historical sites in Pennsylvania (his state), develop a tour guide, e.g. Philadelphia — liberty bell; Gettysburg — Civil War battlefield; Honesdale — Stourbridge Lion.
9. After a field trip through the community, draw a map of it.
10. Given a map, locate his state and local community.
11. Given a map of his state, locate the principle cities.
12. Given a population density map of his state, give reasons for the distribution.
13. Given road maps of his state, chart routes from one given location to another.
14. Given a comparative study of rural and urban parts of his state, list differences in life-style.

ITEM   INSTRUCTIONAL OBJECTIVE

The student is able to . . .

15. Following a discussion of natural resources, list major natural resources in his state.

16. Given a survey of agriculture and industry in his state, point out locations and reasons for the development of each, e.g. Pittsburgh — steel industry — good water transportation.

17. After discussing the importance of water to his state (vary topic according to state), prepare a map showing the principle waterways.

18. Given a discussion of his state's relationship to surrounding states, list five reasons his state is of significant economic importance.

19. After a discussion on recreational opportunities in his state, prepare a vacation guide.

20. Following a discussion of items such as the state flag, bird, and flower, list what each is used for as a state emblem.

21. Given a discussion of local government, distinguish between borough, township, county, etc.

22. After a discussion of the democratic process, explain procedures of an election and participate in a school election.

23. Given instruction in the use of a voting machine, cast a ballot properly.

24. After reviewing newspaper accounts of activities of the governor and state agencies, list five functions of the executive branch of the state government.

25. Given a copy of a current legislative bill, explain how it becomes a law.

26. After a discussion or field trip to the local court and interviews with court personnel, explain the judicial process.

27. After a week's survey of the local newspaper, list local community events.

28. After a week's survey of the newspaper, identify and re-

ITEM   INSTRUCTIONAL OBJECTIVE
_____

The student is able to . . .
      late a specific civic problem.
  29. After a series of discussions on ecology, identify five
      environmental problems, propose solutions, and suggest
      ways of participating in related projects.
  30. After a discussion of community problems, select one
      that interests him and compose a letter to an elected
      official expressing his own opinion.

_____

NATIONAL COMMUNITY
  1. Given biographical studies of several early explorers of
     America, state their accomplishments.
  2. After reviewing settlements in the United States, list col-
     onizing nations and point out the areas they settled.
  3. Given descriptions of life in colonial America, list some
     causes of dissatisfaction that eventually led to the Revo-
     lution.
  4. After studying the Revolutionary War, describe its effects
     on the country.
  5. Discuss some ideals set forth in the Declaration of Inde-
     pendence.
  6. Explain the significance of the United States Constitu-
     tion and list its principle divisions.
  7. After discussing the Bill of Rights, list five rights enjoyed
     as a citizen.
  8. Given maps of the United States between 1776 and the
     present, point out the differences and give reasons for
     them.
  9. After studying the War between the States, list the major
     causes, significant battles, and prominent leaders.
 10. Given charts showing immigration statistics and a dis-
     cussion of socioeconomic conditions of foreign lands,
     give reasons for the large immigration movements.
 11. Given a comparative study of a present-day American
     family and a late nineteenth century American family,

ITEM INSTRUCTIONAL OBJECTIVE

The student is able to . . .

point out differences in their life-styles.

12. After discussing the changing conditions of black Americans since the passage of the thirteenth amendment, identify reasons for and result of the social changes.

13. After a discussion of the problems of minority group members, suggest some proposed solutions.

14. Explain the significance and symbolism of the American flag.

15. Given important historical events in American history, construct a time line.

16. Given a map of the world, trace the boundaries of the United States and identify neighboring countries.

17. Given an outline map of the United States, locate twenty-five states.

18. Given a physical map of the United States, point out significant rivers, lakes, mountains, and plains.

19. Given a climatic map of the United States, describe the general climate in different areas.

20. Given a weather map from a newspaper, determine the weather for a specific area of the United States on that day.

21. Given a physical map of the United States, trace western expansion routes and list geographic reasons for their use.

22. After reviewing the natural resources of the United States, prepare a product map.

23. After discussing the farm areas of the United States, explain why a specific crop is grown in a given region.

24. Given a list of ten major cities of the United States, name one he would like to visit and list things to see there.

25. List the three branches of government and the reason for the separation of powers given in the United States Constitution.

26. Name four cabinet positions and functions in the executive branch of government.

ITEM   INSTRUCTIONAL OBJECTIVE
_____

The student is able to . . .

27. After a discussion of the legislative branch of government, describe generally the process of law making.
28. After a discussion of the judicial branch of government, give examples of court decisions which have affected our lives.
29. After a discussion of major political parties in the United States, identify them and explain their purposes.
30. Given pamphlets describing employment opportunities with the United States Government, explain how the civil service system operates.
31. Given comparative food prices, describe some actions taken by the federal government in pricing.
32. After a discussion on integration, list steps taken by the government to resolve this issue.
33. Given a list of environmental problems, suggest some governmental remedies.
34. Given accounts of poisoning by contaminated food, describe the importance of the work of the Food and Drug Administration.

_____

WORLD COMMUNITY

1. After reading and reviewing material on prehistoric man, discuss the life of the caveman.
2. Given a survey of ancient civilizations, list some of their contributions.
3. After discussing nonwestern civilizations, list several and state accomplishments of each.
4. After studying colonialism, list countries that built empires on colonialism results.
5. After a discussion on democracy, define it and explain its advantages.
6. After reviewing nationalism, define it and state possible results of it.
7. After studying industrialization, identify ways in which

ITEM   INSTRUCTIONAL OBJECTIVE
_____

The student is able to . . .

it has affected our lives.

8. After a review of religions of the world, list four and specify major areas of influence.

9. Given a world map, identify and locate continents and name countries within each.

10. Given a map of the world, locate and name the major oceans.

11. Given a globe of the world, locate the equator and relate how distance north or south affects temperature.

12. Given an atlas, read specialized maps such as population, vegetation, and precipitation.

13. After a review of several countries, describe some ways in which land features and climate affect the people.

14. After discussing the products of selected nations, explain reasons for world trade.

15. After discussing the products of Latin America, visit a local store and compile a list of Latin American products for sale.

16. Given a comparative review of a nation with abundant natural resources and a nation with few, list the effects of each.

17. After reviewing several western European countries, state some geographic reasons why they have developed as industrial powers.

18. After a discussion of several geographical environments, identify how man has modified them for his betterment.

19. Given travel folders from various parts of the world, select an area to visit, prepare an itinerary, select means of travel, and list articles to take on the trip.

20. Given pictures and a discussion on people of the world, state ways in which geographic environment has affected cultures.

21. Given the statement, "The world is growing smaller," state how advanced transportation and communications have affected intercultural relationships.

ITEM	INSTRUCTIONAL OBJECTIVE

The student is able to . . .

22. Explain the purpose of the United Nations and list several of its functions.
23. Given newspapers describing the activities of world leaders, match five leaders with the country each represents.
24. After discussing world problems, list organizations through which governments work for international understanding.
25. Following a discussion of recent natural disasters, explain ways in which they have been alleviated through international cooperation.
26. Given a list of current world problems, suggest and discuss proposed solutions.

UNIT IV

CAREER

AND

VOCATIONAL

SKILLS

THE career and vocational program for the special needs learner was developed to provide a sequential, measurable grouping of skills which will prepare the student for an effective place in the world of work.

Most student trainees engage in a half-day "academic" program and half-day vocational one. The program is for the use of both the teacher and aides. The instructor will use many objectives for skills training; other objectives will lend themselves to both classroom and practical application. Some objectives will be used mostly by the instructional aide in practical

103

areas.

Even with the varied pre-vocational and vocational offerings, it was found that some learners were given little functional pre-vocational training. To this end, the greenhouse and landscaping programs were developed as examples of life planning. Under greenhouse, the student will begin by learning general concepts, proceeding to tools and materials used, and finally learning specific production skills. The instructional objectives in landscaping begin with the use of tools, including layout and planting, and finishes with the maintenance of the landscape. Special emphasis is placed on the actual "doing" of the work rather than the more conceptual levels. Repetitive-type training is highly recommended.

As the learners approach the completion of the program objectives, instructors can channel those with inclination and ability in the direction of specific areas in the world of work.

It is not the purpose of this program to make "master" workers, but to provide an area of vocational competence, or in some instances a single salable skill.

Imagination is essential in developing innovative programs based on the geographic location and available resources, which consider the special needs of the learner.

INSTRUCTIONAL UNIT: WORLD OF WORK

ITEM INSTRUCTIONAL OBJECTIVE

The student is able to . . .
1. Define the term *occupation.*
2. State three reasons why individuals work.
3. Given a specific family situation, state how each family member contributes to the welfare of the group.

   (The following instructional objectives comprise a survey of job and career opportunities. It is recommended that the survey include a class trip, discussion, demonstration, and simulated or actual learner experience.)
4. Given a survey of child care techniques, explain the work of child care workers.
5. Following a survey of hospital work, describe the work of nurse's aids and other hospital workers.
6. After a survey of a supermarket, discuss employment opportunities in the food marketing field.
7. Given a survey of domestic work, list the tasks of a domestic worker.
8. Given a survey of the food preparation and service field, list and describe jobs available in a restaurant.
9. After a survey of the laundry and dry cleaning field, list job opportunities in this field.
10. Given a survey of automobile service and repair, describe work in this area.
11. Following a survey of the building maintenance field, list several jobs of the custodian.
12. Given a survey of office work, list five office machines and their purposes.
13. Given a survey of department stores, role-play a salesperson at work.
14. Following a survey of factory work, participate with others in collating a booklet, using assembly line procedure.
15. Given a survey of the work of painters, carpenters,

ITEM INSTRUCTIONAL OBJECTIVE

The student is able to . . .

    plumbers, and masons, explain why each needs assistants.
16. Given a survey of the field of pet care, take care of a small animal and discuss the procedures involved.
17. Following a survey of the furniture industry, trace the route of a piece of lumber from sawmill to salesroom.
18. Given a survey of local farming, explain the daily routine of a specific farmer.
19. Given a survey of the construction industry, explain the work of an apprentice in the building trades.
20. Given a survey of the civil service, select and describe three civil service jobs that are of interest.
21. Following a survey of the trucking industry, describe the weekly routine of a truck driver.
22. Given a survey of the resort industry, list five seasonal employment opportunities in the area.
23. Given a survey of the baking industry, list several jobs in the field.
24. Given a list of previous school graduates, identify five types of employment in which they are engaged.
25. Given brochures of several vocational schools, list and describe the courses offered.
26. Given the opportunity to talk with someone who has attended a vocational school in another area, state problems associated with living away from home.
27. After a discussion of the military service, list its branches.
28. Given brochures concerning the armed forces, list educational/vocational opportunities offered.
29. Given a brochure of various federal programs, list programs open to him and advantages of each.
30. After a visit to the state employment service, list and explain state programs that offer education or training.

INSTRUCTIONAL UNIT: TELEPHONE SKILLS

ITEM   INSTRUCTIONAL OBJECTIVE

The student will be able to . . .
1. Correctly dial a local telephone number.
2. Given a telephone directory, read and explain the general information section.
3. Using a telephone directory, locate a specific business number.
4. Given the names of three specific individuals, locate their telephone numbers in the directory.
5. Given a long distance telephone number, dial it correctly.
6. Given instructions for using a pay telephone, read and demonstrate them.
7. Use directory assistance to secure a telephone number.
8. Given a problem in using the telephone (such as a wrong number, an out-of-order phone, or a disconnection), explain the problem to the operator.
9. Given the hypothetical situation in which he is unable to keep an appointment, use the telephone to cancel the appointment.
10. Given an emergency situation, use the telephone to summon the assistance of the fire department, police department, or ambulance.

INSTRUCTIONAL UNIT:
MONEY-TAXES-BANKING-INSURANCE

ITEM   INSTRUCTIONAL OBJECTIVE
_____

The student is able to . . .

1. Given a selection of standard American coins and bills, identify them correctly.
2. Given a simulated purchasing situation, make correct change.
3. After a discussion on budgets, state three reasons for preparing a personal budget.
4. Following a discussion of budgets, prepare a personal budget for one week.
5. Given bills from the telephone company, electric company, and a contractor, read and explain them.
6. Explain and illustrate the meaning of the term *debt*.
7. Given a situation in which an individual borrows money, conclude whether the borrowing was appropriate.
8. Given advertisements from banks and finance companies, determine which have lower interest rates.
9. Define and discuss the terms *guaranteed, quality,* and *name brand*.
10. Given simulated purchasing experiences, state reasons for purchasing with cash, by installment, or on layaway.
11. After a discussion concerning trading of automobiles, explain depreciation.
12. Given a sales receipt, explain its use.
13. Given a hypothetical situation in which no taxes are paid, list ten services that would be curtailed.
14. Given a list of specific taxes paid, identify them as to local, state, or federal.
15. Given a discussion of types of taxes, list seven types.
16. Given a pay check stub, identify and explain tax deductions.
17. Given the booklet that explains the federal income tax form, list taxable items.
18. Given an income tax form, list five items requested on

ITEM   INSTRUCTIONAL OBJECTIVE

The student is able to . . .

    the form.

19. Explain the terms *deduction, exemption, gross income, net income,* and *tax withheld.*
20. Complete a tax form correctly.
21. Given a hypothetical situation in which an individual requires help concerning tax forms, suggest sources of assistance.
22. After a discussion of money, state the name and location of the banks in the community.
23. After discussing banks, list the services provided.
24. Given literature from a bank, explain the following: account, deposit, withdrawal, interest, check, loan, dividend, and mortgage.
25. Given a savings passbook, explain the purpose of a savings account.
26. Given savings deposit and withdrawal slips, fill them out correctly.
27. Given a checkbook, explain the purpose of having a checking account.
28. Given a sample check, fill it out correctly.
29. After a discussion of birth certificates and other valuable documents, give reasons for the use of a safe deposit box.
30. Given a situation in which it is necessary to borrow money, list the types of loans available from a bank.
31. Explain the terms *principal* and *interest* in banking.
32. Given a traveler's check, explain how and why it is used.
33. After a discussion concerning the saving of money for special needs, explain the Christmas Club saving plan.
34. Explain the benefits of United States Savings Bonds.
35. Explain how and why credit cards are used.
36. Given the term *insurance,* define it and explain why it is needed.
37. After a discussion or visit to an insurance office, list five types of insurance.
38. Explain the work of an insurance agent and adjuster.

ITEM	INSTRUCTIONAL OBJECTIVE

The student is able to . . .

39. After a discussion reviewing the need for insurance, mention ways insurance can be purchased (directly, through an agent).
40. List types of insurance coverage available for the automobile.
41. Given an automobile insurance application, satisfactorily complete it.
42. Given a hypothetical automobile accident, list things that must be done at the scene.
43. Given a hypothetical automobile accident, complete an accident report form.
44. Explain why people buy life insurance.
45. List and explain five types of life insurance plans.
46. Define and discuss the terms *premium, noncancellable, beneficiary, endowment, and grace period*.
47. Given a newspaper account of a fire, discuss the advantages of having fire insurance.
48. Given an application for health and accident insurance, fill it out correctly.

INSTRUCTIONAL UNIT: LOCATING A JOB

ITEM	INSTRUCTIONAL OBJECTIVE

The student is able to . . .

1. Given a situation in which a person is in need of a job, suggest sources for seeking employment (other people, organizations, and want ads).
2. Given the name of the state employment service, explain its purposes, location, and operation.
3. Compile a list of potential employers in the community.
4. Given a newspaper, locate the classified section.
5. Given the classified section of a newspaper, select an advertised job in which he is interested.
6. Given specific want ads, explain the abbreviations and terms used.
7. Given a specific want ad, evaluate personal suitability to the job.
8. Given a specific job, list expenses connected with the job (eating, transportation, and clothing).
9. Given a specific want ad, simulate answering the ad in person, by telephone, and in writing.
10. Given the term *employment agency*, distinguish between state and private agencies as to cost and service.
11. Given the opportunity to simulate a job interview, come to class appropriately groomed for the specific interview.
12. Given the opportunity for a simulated job interview, come prepared with social security card, application information, pen, etc.
13. Given the location of a job interview, explain how to get to the interview from home.
14. Given a simulated job interview, role-play the interview using appropriate behavior and manners, such as being on time, introducing himself and answering questions courteously.
15. Given samples of signs which appear in employment offices, read and explain them.
16. Given a simulated interview situation, participate cor-

ITEM	INSTRUCTIONAL OBJECTIVE

The student is able to . . .

rectly in the opening, conversation, and conclusion of the interview.

17. Given specific questions concerning personal background reply appropriately.

18. Given a specific job, discuss and evaluate its implications in the following areas: working alone vs. with others, standing vs. sitting, variety vs. sameness, manual vs. intellectual labor, nights vs. days, and indoors vs. outdoors.

19. Given an application form, explain its purpose and complete it correctly.

20. Given the term *work-study*, explain the program as it exists in his own school.

21. Given the possibility of participating in the work-study program, list the prerequisites for the program, such as age, insurance, attitude, and achievement.

22. Given disagreeable situations which arise during employment, role-play possible solutions.

23. Given a list of work-study employers in the area, describe the employment opportunities at each.

24. Given information regarding work-study salaries, state reasons why they are below salaries of regular employees.

25. Given an introduction to the supervisor of work-study, state ways in which the individual will assist him.

INSTRUCTIONAL UNIT: EMPLOYMENT

ITEM INSTRUCTIONAL UNIT

The student is able to . . .

1. Following a discussion concerning the first day on a new job, state five things that should be remembered.
2. After a discussion concerning the first day on a new job, list three areas with which he must be familiar (lunchroom, restroom, exits, supervisor's station).
3. Given an hourly rate of pay, compute the weekly salary.
4. Following a discussion concerning gross and net pay, list items deducted from the salary.
5. Given a list of itemized deductions and gross salary, determine net salary.
6. Distinguish between the terms hourly and weekly rate of pay.
7. Given a list of jobs, select those for which licensing or a civil service examination is required.
8. List the fringe benefits of a selected job.
9. Given various means of transportation to a given job, list factors for consideration in determining the most appropriate means.
10. Given one-way cost of transportation to work, compute the weekly cost.
11. Given the starting time of a job and the amount of travel time involved, determine when he must leave home to arrive on time for work.
12. Given a bus or train schedule, determine what time a given bus or train will arrive at a given location.
13. After a discussion of responsibility on the job, list five characteristics of a responsible worker.
14. Following a discussion of safety on the job, state three reasons why safety is important.
15. Given a specific shop task, state several safety rules related to the task.
16. Given a list of danger warning signs, read and react appropriately to them.

ITEM	INSTRUCTIONAL OBJECTIVE

The student is able to . . .

17. Given a specified job, list safety equipment to be used in the performance of that job.
18. Given a specific job, list and describe appropriate clothing for the safe performance of that job.
19. After discussing safety devices such as machine guards, aprons, safety shoes, work gloves, and glasses, explain the value of these items.
20. After discussing a job location, point out the specific location of the fire alarm, fire extinguishers, first aid kits, and emergency exits.
21. Given a job accident situation, take the basic steps necessary to get help.
22. Given a simulated accident situation, complete an accident report form.

INSTRUCTIONAL UNIT: HOME MANAGEMENT

ITEM	INSTRUCTIONAL OBJECTIVE

The student is able to . . .

1. Given a specific income, determine the amount that can be spent on housing.
2. Given a lease, read and discuss the details.
3. Given a situation in which a house is rented, list services needed by the tenants (gas, heat, electricity, water, trash removal, etc.).
4. Given a specific rental property, list services furnished by the landlord.
5. After a discussion of several rental properties, list the advantages of each.
6. After a discussion on buying vs. renting, list the advantages of each.
7. Given a simulated situation in which a home is purchased, list the cost involved (down payment, closing costs, mortgage payments, etc.).
8. List several types of home construction.
9. Given a check list of items such as roof, windows, siding, and foundation, describe the condition of a specific home.
10. Given a property tax notice, read it and state its purpose.
11. Given two property tax notices, list five possible reasons why one might be higher than the other.
12. Following a discussion on methods of heating a house, give advantages of each method.
13. After discussing the importance of water to a household, explain how homeowners obtain water.
14. Given a situation in which electric lights fail to function, suggest possible reasons for such failure.
15. Given the term *maintenance,* define it and explain why it is an essential part of home ownership.
16. After discussing the effects of winter weather, list four problems of home ownership during that season (snow removal, heating, storm windows, roofing, etc.).
17. Following a discussion of the effects of spring on a

ITEM   INSTRUCTIONAL OBJECTIVE
_____

The student is able to . . .

house identify five tasks facing the homeowner each spring (cleaning, garden and lawn care, etc.).

18. After a discussion of summer activities, list four concerns of the homeowner in summer.

19. Following a discussion of the changing weather in autumn, list three concerns of the homeowner during this season.

20. Given statistics on home accidents, list five danger areas in the home and what to do about them.

INSTRUCTIONAL UNIT: LEISURE AND RECREATION

ITEM   INSTRUCTIONAL OBJECTIVE

The student is able to . . .
1. Explain the terms *leisure* and *recreation* as applied to life.
2. Given the opportunity to observe a spectator sport, state the recreational advantages.
3. Given the opportunity to participate in a sport such as softball or basketball, state the recreational advantages.
4. Given a leisure time period and a list of leisure activities, select a recreational activity in which to engage.
5. After explaining the word *hobby*, list six hobbies.
6. Given descriptions of several hobbies, report to the class on one of them.
7. Given a specific community, list three organizations or clubs in which he is eligible for membership.
8. Given a specific organization in which he is interested, state the purpose, dues, meeting place, and rules of the organization.
9. Given some travel folders, select a place he would like to visit and describe it to the class.
10. Given a road map, chart a route from home community to a nearby point of interest.
11. Given the opportunity for a picnic, select an appropriate park location and list reasons for the choice.
12. Given the opportunity for a class outing, make plans for the following: transportation, menu, activities, and specific cost.

Unit V

INNOVATIVE

TRAINING

PROGRAMS

INSTRUCTIONAL UNIT: GREENHOUSE

ITEM   INSTRUCTIONAL OBJECTIVE
_____

The student is able to . . .
1. Following a discussion and introduction to a greenhouse facility, give the general purpose of associated work.
2. After a discussion concerning plant growth and environment, relate the need of the controlled greenhouse environment.
3. After discussing the importance of the controlled greenhouse environment, locate and read thermometers.
4. Given a thermometer reading, adjust the thermostat, open windows, or make other environmental controls to specifications.
5. Given a tour of the greenhouse and discussion of various plants and flowers, recognize plants grown for beauty and those grown to produce food.
6. Given various plants and flowers, recognize and name them correctly.
7. After a discussion concerning the importance of the electrical system in a greenhouse, recognize malfunctioning equipment and report it to the instructor.
8. Following an inspection of greenhouse beds and benches, check them to determine if repairs are needed and to make necessary repairs under supervision.
9. Shown a display of various greenhouse tools, recognize and name them.
10. Given various greenhouse tools, state safety precautions to be remembered when using each tool.
11. Given various greenhouse tools, state what they are used for and demonstrate uses.
12. Given various greenhouse tools, clean and store them properly.
13. Given a demonstration in glass cleaning, properly clean a glass window.
14. After discussing the danger of working around glass, list safety precautions.

ITEM	INSTRUCTIONAL OBJECTIVE

The student is able to . . .

15. After a discussion concerning plant infection by disease, state hygienic measures to be remembered.
16. Following an examination of greenhouse plants, locate the root systems and state their importance.
17. After an examination of greenhouse plants, recognize the stem and state its importance.
18. After an examination of greenhouse plants, recognize the leaf and flower and state their importance.
19. Given the ingredients contained in greenhouse soil, mix the soil properly.
20. Given greenhouse soil, take the necessary steps for sterilization.
21. Given various types of pots, identify them as to composition.
22. Given various types of pots, choose the proper pot for various types of plants.
23. Given used pots, wash the pots correctly.
24. Given pots and soil, place the soil in the pots.
25. Given plant seeds and planting pots, plant the seeds.
26. Given a healthy plant, properly take cuttings.
27. Given plant cuttings, correctly place them in the propagation bench.
28. Given a healthy cutting in the propagation bench, transplant it to the proper pot.
29. Given potted plants, check by touching soil to see if the plants need water.
30. Given various potted plants, water them correctly.
31. Following a discussion of plant growth, state why fertilizer is used.
32. After discussing fertilizer, state safety precautions with its use.
33. Correctly fertilize plants with a dry fertilizer.
34. Mix dry fertilizer with water for use.
35. Given fertilizer mixed with water, correctly feed the plants.

ITEM   INSTRUCTIONAL OBJECTIVE
_____

The student is able to . . .

36. Given examples of plants with diseases, correctly identify common plant diseases.

37. Name an insecticide to be used with a diseased plant.

38. Given plants with various diseases, prepare and administer the correct treatment under supervision.

39. Following a demonstration in transplanting, correctly transplant various plants.

40. After a demonstration in pinching, correctly pinch plants.

41. Following a demonstration in disbudding plants, disbud them correctly.

42. Harvest mature flowers for sale.

43. Sort cut flowers for marketing.

44. Grade various types of cut flowers for marketing.

45. Bunch flowers for marketing.

46. Pack various flowers for shipment.

47. Properly store various types of cut flowers.

48. Arrange and transplant various kinds of potted plants to ornamental pots for retail sale.

(Objectives 49 through 78 were prepared for student production of chrysanthemums and tomatoes. Chrysanthemums were chosen as an example of a plant grown to produce flowers for retail sale; tomatoes were chosen as a vegetable grown for sale as a plant.)

49. Following a discussion concerning the importance of a clean bench for planting, prepare the benches.

50. Correctly mix planting soil by mixing one-third peat, one-third perlite or sand, and one-third topsoil.

51. Mix bone meal, lime, superphosphate, and 5-10-5 fertilizer in the soil.

52. Following a discussion concerning the necessity and method of sterilization, state safety precautions such as wearing gloves, boots, and apron and being careful with hot water.

ITEM	INSTRUCTIONAL OBJECTIVE

The student is able to . . .

53. Given soil to sterilize, correctly sterilize it, using water about 200° Fahrenheit.
54. Plant seedlings in the proper place using mesh guides.
55. After discussing the necessity of maintaining a healthy root system and soil, mix and apply Terrachlor® and Captan® to the soil.
56. Check the soil and water the chrysanthemum seedlings when needed.
57. After discussing fertilization of mums, state the type of fertilizer to use (20-20-20), mix it with water, state how often it should be applied (once a week for seven weeks, once every two weeks after seven weeks old), and correctly apply it.
58. After a discussion concerning show mums, pick the suckers daily, giving the reason why this is necessary to create large crown flowers.
59. Following a discussion concerning continuing bench cleanliness, weed the benches and keep possible contaminating materials away from the area.
60. Cut mature mums for sale.
61. Place the cut mums in water containers to retain freshness.
62. Wrap the cut mums in wax paper and staple the corners for shipment.
63. After discussing the use of special seeds for planting tomatoes, list the reasons for use of certified seeds.
64. Properly mix planting soil by mixing one-third peat, one-third perlite or sand, and one-third top soil.
65. Mix the correct type of fertilizer for tomato plants in the soil.
66. Place the planting soil in a flat.
67. Following a discussion concerning the necessity and method of sterilization, list safety precautions to follow.
68. Sterilize soil using water about 200° Fahrenheit.
69. Given sterilized soil in planting pots, use a pegboard to

ITEM   **INSTRUCTIONAL OBJECTIVE**

The student is able to . . .
    make the holes for planting seed.

70. Given a flat of soil with properly spaced planting holes, place the seed in the hole and cover with about one-fourth inch of soil.
71. Place the flats with planted seeds on a bench and cover with plastic or glass to aid germination.
72. Given flats covered with plastic, check the seeds each day for germination so that the plastic may be removed immediately upon germination to prevent stringy plants and damping-off.
73. Given germinated tomato plants, place them in direct sunlight in an area away from other greenhouse plants to prevent transfer of plant parasites.
74. After discussing the necessity of maintaining a healthy root system and soil, mix and apply Terrachlor and Captan to the soil.
75. Check the soil and water the tomato seedlings when needed.
76. Correctly fertilize the tomato plants.
77. After demonstrating where to look for plant parasites, examine plants and determine if parasites are present.
78. Given several week-old tomato plants, place flats outside (when weather is warm enough) to adjust to environment.

INSTRUCTIONAL UNIT: LANDSCAPING

ITEM	INSTRUCTIONAL OBJECTIVE

The student is able to . . .

1. Given various tools used for landscaping and maintenance, identify a rake, shovel, pruner, lawn mower, edger, trimmer, spreader, and roller.
2. Choose the proper shovel for various types of work.
3. Choose the proper rake for a specific job.
4. Choose the proper pruning tool to be used on roses, shrubs, and hedges.
5. Choose the proper tools used in lawn care (mower, hedger, and trimmer).
6. Correctly clean various tools used in landscape maintenance after their use.
7. Properly store tools used in landscape maintenance.
8. Following instruction in the use of a ruler or yardstick, measure in inches, half inches, and quarter inches.
9. Given pint containers, quart containers, and various sizes of buckets, fill the proper container with water as requested by the instructor.
10. Given a 100 foot tape measure, correctly measure and lay out an outside garden.
11. Given a newly established landscape, recognize the significance of maintaining the topsoil.
12. Given a newly established landscape, discuss the significance of taking soil samples for testing.
13. Given a newly established landscape, prepare the topsoil for planting.
14. Given trees or shrubs to be planted, differentiate between bareroot and balled stock to be planted.
15. State the preferred time of the year for planting nursery stock.
16. Soak the root system of a tree or shrub and state why this is important.
17. Dig a hole to plant a tree or shrub.
18. Spread the tree or shrub roots for proper planting.
19. Pack the soil around the tree or shrub firmly and water

ITEM INSTRUCTIONAL OBJECTIVE

The student is able to . . .

it.

20. Cut one-fourth to one-third off the lateral branches of a tree or shrub and explain why this is necessary.

21. Given balled shrubs to plant, handle them properly for planting.

22. Correctly plant balled trees or shrubs by digging the proper size of hole, watering, opening the top of the burlap, filling in the hole to the proper depth, and pruning, when necessary.

23. Single stake newly planted trees with less than a two inch trunk for support.

24. Stake newly planted trees with over a two inch trunk with three or four guy wires for support.

25. Place a rubber hose to protect the trunk where a guy wire touches the newly planted tree.

26. State why a trench is the most advantageous method of planting a hedge and then correctly perform the task.

27. Plant clinging vines.

28. Given planted clinging vines, attach them by tying, using buttons or small hooks.

29. Given various common herbacious plants, correctly identify each by name.

30. Given various plants and flowers to be planted in a specific area, lay out, plant, and arrange according to size, coloration, and maintenance.

31. Given annuals, state the time of year they must be planted outside and then properly plant and/or transplant to pots for indoor use.

32. Given perennials (plants or bulbs), give the time of year to plant and then plant the bulbs with the pointed part up when timing is proper.

33. Aid in laying sod for turf in a newly established landscape.

34. Prepare the topsoil for planting grass on a newly established landscape.

ITEM	INSTRUCTIONAL OBJECTIVE

The student is able to . . .

35. Sow the grass seed.

36. Cover the grass seed with soil and water the newly sown yard.

37. Following a discussion concerning shrubs, give four reasons for pruning them.

38. Given trees or shrubs to prune, assemble the correct tools for the job.

39. State safety precautions when pruning trees or shrubs.

40. Cut a matured shrub to ground level to rejuvenate it.

41. Prune a shrub with uneven growth by "heading back" to improve form.

42. Remove the dead shoots on a rose plant and prune to twelve inches.

43. Given a shrub, examine it for injured parts.

44. Given a shrub with injured branches, remove injured part above a strong lateral on the shrub.

45. Wrap or paint the injured part of a shrub to prevent disease.

46. Recognize and correctly remove the suckers on a grafted tree.

47. Correctly state the time of year for pruning shade trees.

48. Prune shade trees to remove undesirable growth such as water sprouts, rubbing branches, broken limbs, and suckers.

49. Examine various shrubs for fertilizer deficiency by looking for undersized leaves, yellow or chlorotic leaves, and sparse foliage.

50. Take a soil sample for analysis to determine the proper fertilizer to apply to a lawn or shrub.

51. Fertilize a lawn using a fertilizer spreader, taking the precautions to water immediately after spreading to prevent fertilizer burn.

52. Fertilize trees by placing fertilizer in twelve- to- eighteen inch holes about two inches in diameter around the base.

53. Following a discussion concerning the use of mulch

ITEM   INSTRUCTIONAL OBJECTIVE
_____

The student is able to . . .

around shrubs, state the reasons for its use, such as to conserve moisture, prevent runoff, keep more even soil temperature, and control weeds.

54. Identify by sight peat moss, sawdust, corncobs, and wood chips as materials used for mulching.

55. Given mulch and planted shrubs, correctly place the mulch around the base of the shrub.

56. Plant patchwork grass, correctly covering it with the proper covering agent.

57. Correctly weed a garden manually.

58. Given a yard to mow, use a manual or power mower to cut the grass.

THE SPECIAL NEEDS LEARNER

AGENCIES PROVIDING SERVICES/RESOURCES

Allergy Foundation of America
801 Second Ave.
New York, N.Y. 10017

American Foundation for the Blind
15 West 16th St.
New York, N.Y. 10010

American Psychiatric Association
Publications Office
1700 18th St., N.W.
Washington, D.C. 20009

American Psychological Association
1200 17th St., N.W.
Washington, D.C. 20036

Bureau of Education for the Handicapped
United States Office of Education
Department of Health, Education, and Welfare
Washington, D.C. 20202

Children's Bureau Publication
Superintendent of Documents
U.S. Government Printing Office
Department of Health, Education and Welfare
Washington, D.C. 20402

Collier-Macmillan Paperbacks
Collier Books
866 Third Ave.
New York, N.Y. 10022

The Council for Exceptional Children
1920 Association Drive
Reston, Va. 22091

Eastern Pennsylvania Regional Resources Center for Special Education (RRC)
1013 West Ninth Ave.
King of Prussia, Pa. 19406

Epilepsy Foundation of America
1729 F St., N.W.
Washington, D.C. 20005

League for Emotionally Disturbed Children
171 Madison Ave.
New York, N.Y. 10017

Metropolitan Life Insurance Co.
Health and Welfare Division
1 Madison Ave.
New York, N.Y. 10010

Myklebust, H. R.
The Volta Bureau
1537 35th St., N.W.
Washington, D.C. 20402

National Association for Mental Health
10 Columbus Circle
New York, N.Y. 10019

National Congress of Parents and Teachers
700 N. Rush St.
Chicago, Ill. 60611

National Cystic Fibrosis Research Foundation
521 Fifth Ave.
New York, N.Y. 10017

National Education Association
1201 16th St., N.W.
Washington, D.C. 20036

The National Foundation — March of Dimes
800 Second Ave.
New York, N.Y. 10017

National Society for Autistic Children
621 Central Ave.
Albany, N.Y. 12206

National Society for Crippled Children and Adults
2023 W. Ogden Ave.
Chicago, Ill. 60612

Pennsylvania Society for Crippled Children and Adults
1107 N. Front St.
Box 1297
Harrisburg, Pa. 17108

Department of Public Health
Division of Maternal and Child Health Services
Washington, D.C. 20402

Public Affairs Pamphlets
381 Park Ave. South
New York, N.Y. 10016

Public Health Service Publication
U.S. Department of Health, Education and Welfare
Superintendent of Documents
U.S. Government Printing Office
Washington, D.C. 20402

United Cerebral Palsy Association, Inc.
321 W. 44th St.
New York, N.Y. 10036

U.S. Department of Health, Education and Welfare
Public Health Service
4040 N. Fairfax Drive
Arlington, Va. 22203

RELATED LITERATURE*

About Children With Cleft . . . .Pennsylvania Society for
Lips and Cleft Palates   Crippled Children and
                                       Adults

---

*Addresses for publishers are listed under Services/Resources.

Birth Defect: The Tragedy and the Hope . . . .The National Foundation — March of Dimes

Birth Defects: Question and Answers . . . .The National Foundation — March of Dimes

Birth Defects Treatment Center . . . .The National Foundation — March of Dimes

Caring For Your Disabled Child (Spock, B.) . . . .Collier-Macmillan

Cerebral Palsy: More Hope Than Ever . . . .Public Affairs Pamphlets, No. 40

Cerebral Palsy: What You Should Know About It . . . .United Cerebral Palsy Associations, Inc.

The Child Who Is Hard of Hearing . . . .Children's Bureau Publications, No. 36

The Child With Cerebral Palsy . . . .Children's Bureau Publications, No. 34

The Child With a Cleft Palate . . . .Children's Bureau Publications, No. 36

The Child With Epilepsy . . . .Children's Bureau Publications, No. 35

The Child With Missing Arm or Leg . . . .Children's Bureau Publications, No. 49

The Child With Rheumatic Fever . . . .Children's Bureau Publications, No. 42

The Child With a Speech Problem . . . .Children's Bureau Publications, No. 52

Choosing A Hearing Aid . . . .Children's Bureau Publications, No. 55

Congenital Malformations: The Problem and the Task . . . .The National Foundation — March of Dimes

Conquer Cystic Fibrosis: Questions and Answers . . . .National Cystic Fibrosis Research Foundation

Don't Gamble With the Future: Epilepsy	. . . .U.S. Department of Health, Education, and Welfare
Epilepsy: Recognition, Onset, Diagnosis, and Therapy	. . . .Epilepsy Foundation of America
Facts About Blindness	. . . .American Foundation for the Blind
For Nurses: Cystic Fibrosis	. . . .National Cystic Fibrosis Research Foundation
How To Help Your Handicapped Child	. . . .Public Affairs Pamphlets, No. 219
Is My Baby All Right? (Apgar, V. and Beck, J.)	. . . .Trident Press (Div. of Simon & Schuster 630 Fifth Ave. New York, N.Y. 10020)
Is Your Child Blind?	. . . .American Foundation for the Blind
Kidney Disease	. . . .Public Health Service, Pub. No. 1307
Living With Cystic Fibrosis, A Guide for the Young Adult	. . . .National Cystic Fibrosis Research Foundation
Memo to Parents About Your Child's Eyesight	. . . .Metropolitan Life
Questions and Answers About Cerebral Palsy	. . . .United Cerebral Palsy Associations Inc.
A Teacher's Guide to Cystic Fibrosis	. . . .National Cystic Fibrosis Research Foundation
Training Aphasic Children (Myklebust, H. R.)	. . . .H. R. Myklebust

What About a Child With a Cleft Palate?	. . .	.Department of Public Health, Division of Maternal Child Health Services
When Your Child Has Rheumatoid Arthritis	. . .	.The National Foundation — March of Dimes
You Are Not Alone: Help For Your Crippled Child	. . .	.National Society for Crippled Children and Adults
You, Your Child, and Epilepsy	. . .	.Epilepsy Foundation of America
Your Child and Cystic Fibrosis	. . .	.National Cystic Fibrosis Research Foundation
Your Pre-School Child's Eyes	. . .	.Children's Bureau Publications, No. 54

INDEX